The Writer's
QUICK-START GUIDE

(Revised And Expanded Edition)

Modern **Know-How** To
Supercharge
Your **Creative**
Writing

BRENDAN LLOYD

Copyright © 2023 Brendan Lloyd

ISBN: 978-1-922788-30-6
Published by Vivid Publishing
A division of Fontaine Publishing Group
P.O. Box 948, Fremantle
Western Australia 6959
www.vividpublishing.com.au

 A catalogue record for this book is available from the National Library of Australia

Second edition. All rights reserved. No part of this publication may be reproduced, stored in a retrieval system or transmitted in any form or by any means, electronic, mechanical, photocopying, recording or otherwise, without the prior written permission of the copyright holder.

Contents

Introduction 1

What To Expect And Not Expect 4
From The Creative Industry

Write (Better) Stuff 13

Contemplating Comedy 35

Japanese Creative Quirkiness 43

Creative Affirmations 49

Mini-Dictionary 69

Writing Tips 78

Polish Plans and
Replacement Episodes Plan 107

Logline And Synopsis 111

Creativity Prayers 115

Introduction

As of the time of writing, I'm a 33-year-old writer, from Australia. I've written three spirituality books, *Out of This World*, *The Om Contemplations*, and *The Prayer Preparer: Practical Prayers For Positive People*.

As for creative writing, I've been working on various 'projects' (or 'franchises'/ 'I.Ps' (Intellectual Properties) if you prefer) for about 14 years, and I've learned many skills and techniques on my own through trial-and-error – skills and techniques I've chosen to share in this book.

It may sound strange to you, the reader, that a writer who hasn't had any original creative works produced would be sharing writing advice, but I was doing creative writing for nearly a decade (since around 2005) before I wrote even my first book. You may not have seen any of my creative projects produced, or read any of my creative work, but skills and techniques I've learned and advice I can provide aspiring writers – particularly those who are 'starting out', especially those who are still in High School or who have recently completed High

School – are still valid. You'll get the most benefit from this book if you are a writer who's still in High School. If you're in late Primary School, even more so.

If you *are* an aspiring writer, you will benefit from advice I was never given by anyone and you will benefit from my knowledge of how the creative industry *actually* operates, which again, was something I was not told until around 2017 by someone I emailed, by which point that knowledge was of little use to me.

This book is written from a Western writer's perspective, so certain information may not be relevant for writers living in Japan (if this book ever gets translated into Japanese – 'konnichiwa!' to any Japanese writers reading this book!), and some information may only be relevant to writers living in the United States.

I'm an Australian writer, and being from an English-speaking country, there's hardly any language barrier between the United States and Australia, which means I can contemplate pursuing creative opportunities in the United States. If you're Japanese, stick to the domestic Japanese creative industry – you have more opportunities when it comes to manga then many/most Western countries have when it comes to comic books and any TV show or movie adaptations.

In the West, you'd virtually have to work for one of the big comic book companies like Marvel or DC to get your own comic book series published, and TV show and movie adaptations of comic books are usually entirely dominated by Marvel and DC. In Japan, almost anyone with sufficient artistic talent can create a manga, and even some mildly successful or obscure manga get adapted into anime – not so in the West.

If you live in virtually any country other than the U.S or Japan, do the best you can with your home country's creative industry, but consider the United States as a backup plan (if you're from a non-English speaking country, be prepared to learn English. If your English is poor, the language barrier may lock you out of opportunities in the United States. Be prepared for difficulties – many writers struggle even without a language barrier to worry about)!

Now, the show, er, *book* must go on!

What To Expect And Not Expect From The Creative Industry

The creative industry, who you plan to work with if you're aspiring to be a writer. All you need is hard work and talent, and the rest sorts itself out, right? Well, maybe not.

You might think you just make a few enquiries until you find the right person – sometimes get rejected but sometimes find someone who's interested. The reality is far bleaker for unproduced writers, so brace yourself.

Something you should keep in mind at all times is that unproduced writers should expect 95% of enquiries to agents, screenwriting managers and producers to receive no response at all. It's nothing personal, that's completely normal for the industry if you're an unproduced writer.

The remaining 5% of enquiries will generally either be a carefully worded PR response for why they're not interested or can't read your submission, or if you're extremely lucky, someone who's interested in one of your projects.

You should not expect to receive many requests to read

a script, and even if you do, you might not get an Option Agreement to produce that project, you might only get feedback about your script (which is still progress – count yourself lucky if you even get *that* far!).

If you do only get feedback, other agents/screenwriting managers/producers might be willing to read your script, due to gatekeepers networking with each other. It's possible, particularly if you received feedback about your script and then made significant improvements to it, that one of the agents/screenwriting managers or producers who reads your script after that might offer you an Option Agreement.

There are several reasons why it's so difficult to receive a response, let alone a script read request, but the main ones are:

1. The creative industry being cautious and risk-averse in relation to a. original projects/franchises b. an unproduced writer
2. Wanting to avoid the possibility of being sued for stealing ideas from a rejected submission
3. The vast majority of scripts from unproduced writers are terrible and they don't want to take a chance on potentially reading a solid or even great script but risk reading another terrible script from timewasters (writers who are inexperienced, lack talent, or are unwilling to fully commit to writing)
4. An original project with too high of a budget that's considered an unacceptable risk

Complicating the matter of receiving script read requests is that some creative companies and even some producers will openly state on their website that they won't accept submissions except through an agent or manager ('manager' referring to screenwriting managers, who apparently mentor writers, help them to improve their scripts, etc). You should definitely make every possible effort to get an agent or screenwriting manager. You might succeed without one, but it would require a *lot* of luck.

Something you should definitely avoid is having the first project you approach the creative industry with being an original Sci-Fi or Fantasy movie. This is because Sci-Fi and fantasy tend to be big budget, and with no name recognition and coming from an unproduced writer, it's highly likely the industry won't take you seriously or otherwise consider your work too high risk.

You would have a much greater chance of getting a Sci-Fi or Fantasy novel published, and a novel would be far less risky and have fewer restrictions. Unless there are reasons why your original Sci-Fi or Fantasy I.P (Intellectual Property) would only work as a movie, TV series or video game (presumably due to limitations of the written format, such as lack of sound, or lack of interactivity), then at least *consider* novels before attempting movies.

Keep in mind that fewer original movies are being produced by Hollywood nowadays, particularly with the COVID situation (this might improve in a few years with higher vaccination rates, but will probably continue to be an issue). Hollywood is mostly producing sequels, prequels, reboots, remakes, spin-offs, movies based on video games, movies based on books, movies based on graphic novels/ comic books/manga – essentially anything with a 'built-in audience' in order to reduce risk. While some streaming services, such as Netflix, produce original movies, an agent or manager is generally a prerequisite if you want to pursue those opportunities.

In terms of ranking the different creative media (novels, movie, TV series, video game, graphic novel/comic book) from easiest to get produced to hardest, I would rank novels and graphic novels as similar (with graphic novels as the more difficult of the two), followed by movies, followed by TV series, followed by video game. Your experiences may be different, you might find graphic novels to be almost as difficult to get produced as video games.

You should more or less expect original video game I.Ps to be the hardest to get produced. One of the reasons for that is that video game writers (sometimes called Lead Writer) often have some other role with the developer and then get assigned or promoted to writer, and another reason is depending on complexity, video games generally take 2-3 years to develop (some RPGs [Role-Playing Games] have been known to take 5 years or more) and the game developer would be taking a risk until the game released and they were able to tell if the game was successful or not, so you can understand that they'd choose already well established writers.

There are very few examples where a writer approached a video game developer and managed to get an original I.P produced, and far more examples of TV series and movies that a writer got produced.

From my understanding of how the creative industry operates in relation to writers (since virtually every assumption

I made about the creative industry was disproven), the main ways the creative industry 'discovers' new writers, at least in the U.S, are:
1. A script that received a 7 or higher on The Black List
2. Being introduced to a writer by someone the agent/manager/producer already knew in the industry
3. A writer produced their own movie (don't attempt this even if your movie is ultra-low budget [$250,000 budget or less], as an unproduced writer it's highly unlikely you could afford it)
4. The writer placed highly in a major writing contest (generally quarterfinals or better)

It's almost depressing that there seems to be so few ways that gatekeepers discover promising new writers, but from what I've been told and online research I've done, that is apparently the 'reality' of succeeding as a writer (at least regarding movies and TV shows) unless you get *extremely* lucky.

As I mentioned earlier, novels are probably much easier to succeed with due to budget being irrelevant and the main cost being publishing costs. The best things to keep in mind when writing novels, in regards to publishers, is to make sure the publisher you're contacting publishes in that genre (approaching a children's book publisher with a fantasy series is virtually guaranteed to end in rejection), and pay close attention to pacing – according to the Wikipedia article about narrative pacing, the most common reason for a novel to be rejected is due to slow pacing.

If you have your heart firmly set on writing video games, play games in the same genre for research and avoid a video game I.P that's too similar to something already in development by a particular developer – that will get you rejection instantly. Also, some video game developers, such as EA, will only accept video game pitches if you've already been working for them for several years. Sorry to shatter your hopes of writing video games, but it's better that you never get your hopes up like I did and have to deal with the crushing disappointment.

If you're determined to write movies, strongly consider writing ultra-low budget movies (budget of less than $250,000) first as a way of potentially breaking-in and being a produced writer, and therefore, *relevant* in the eyes of the industry.

Make sure that if you *do* approach the movie industry with a script, that:

1. It's as high quality as you're capable of writing (and ideally has been tweaked since the completion of the first draft – do *not* send your first draft unless you can't find any way of tweaking it)
2. It's not the first script you've ever written (you would have far too little experience to write a solid, marketable script)
3. It's relatively original
4. The length of the script is 100 pages or less – I've heard that agents/screenwriting managers/producers will be unwilling to read scripts from unproduced writers that are over 100 pages in length. Writing a script as long as one of the Lord of the Rings movies when you're an unproduced writer would be a massive red flag to the creative industry.

Writing TV show scripts is a good way of gaining writing experience, since the quality of your writing should improve.

Your later scripts should tend to have significantly better writing than your earlier ones, and you can always return to your earlier TV show scripts later and tweak them to bring them closer to the quality of your most recent scripts. Do ***not***, however, expect much success in getting script read requests for your original TV series unless you've had success with getting something else produced first that was at least mildly commercially successful (commercial success seems to count for *much* more than critical success).

One thing I should warn you about: if you're writing a novel, do *not* use lyrics to any pre-existing songs (as in, any lyrics you didn't write yourself) without permission from the copyright holder of those songs or you might be open to lawsuits from the music industry – I wanted to use a single line from Michael Jackson's 'Heal the World' as a mantra in *The Om Contemplations* (a non-fiction book), but the publisher insisted that there must be no lyrics in the book at all unless I had permission from the copyright holder(s). It might be difficult to track down the copyright holders for certain songs, and you might have to wait several weeks before even getting a response, and if they do give you permission to use the desired lyrics, they might expect a certain amount of commission from the sale of each copy of the book.

If a song is Public Domain, you won't need permission to use it, but most Public Domain songs are about a hundred years old. When writing TV show, movie, or video game scripts, don't worry about asking permission for including lyrics – I assume when the project enters production, the legal department would obtain all the necessary permissions for any songs you used, whereas when you're writing a novel, you have to request permission for using lyrics yourself. I base this assumption on the fact that movie credits will itemise every song they use, so they must have obtained permission to use them.

Before you make a final decision about whether or not to be a writer, make sure you're choosing to be a writer for the right reasons (such as for the joy of writing and the satisfaction of making 'creative breakthroughs') rather than for fame and/or wealth so that you save yourself a *lot* of disappointment and never get your hopes so high that there's almost no way any amount of success will ever be enough.

A final warning about what to expect or not expect from the creative industry: do *not* hold any hopes or aspirations of:
1. Having a manga, anime, or video game produced in Japan
2. Collaborating with any Japanese writers
3. Moving to Japan to work with a Japanese creative company.

For non-Japanese to have even a remote chance of working with the Japanese on anything creative, you'd probably have to be introduced to a particular individual or company, which would only be remotely possible later in your writing career.

Try to have realistic expectations of the industry when you're making enquiries, and keep writing no matter how many rejections or 'no response routine' reactions you receive. Know what to expect and what not to expect, and you'll get more satisfaction from writing.

With your expectations hopefully set *quite* low, now you can get on with the actual writing and portfolio-building!

Write (Better) Stuff

Now that we've established how high, er, *low*, to set your expectations, you can get to the task of building up a portfolio of creative works, and hopefully one day 'established' is exactly what you'll be as a writer.

Something that will help your writing ability to is do lots of reading. Make every effort to read plenty of books, not just fiction, but also non-fiction. Reading fiction books might give you inspiration for plot, and give you an idea of narrative pace, but reading non-fiction books will give you an idea of how to write in-universe non-fiction (including things like newspapers and 'fake' non-fiction books which are technically fiction (as events and characters might be completely fictional) but are treated in-universe [within the setting of your creative project] as non-fiction.

This style of 'fictional non-fiction' (if you don't mind the phrase) can be especially useful for writing in-universe non-fiction for video games. This would include in-game documents such as newspapers, diaries, non-fiction books [fictional ones], letters, magazines, etc, and even forms of in-universe non-fiction such as audio tapes, CDs, radio broadcasts, fictional in-universe television shows, emails, etc. All of these can be used to further the lore and mythos of the setting, as well as develop character backstories, particularly for characters with few or brief appearances.

I would recommend only attempting to write a video game script once you have **at least** 5 years of writing experience, preferably 10 years of writing experience, especially if you want to work on an RPG.

With anything less than 5 years of writing experience, you'd probably be embarrassing yourself if you tried approaching a video game developer requesting to write a video game script and setting yourself up for rejection. Be prepared for original video game projects and I.Ps/franchises to be the most difficult of your projects to get produced.

I would also recommend that you have **at least** 5 years of writing experience before attempting comedic projects. If you attempt comedic projects with less than 5 years of writing experience, you'll likely fall into the trap of a lot of your humour being lame puns or otherwise attempts at comedy that fall flat or that have stale humour. I will discuss comedic writing in greater detail in the next chapter.

Short stories can be excellent writing practice as you have to be succinct. However, writing a good or excellent short story is probably much harder than writing a good or excellent novel, since a short story often has strict page or word limits (at least if being entered into a competition) while a novel has few page or word restrictions and a novel has the potential to be part of a larger series while a short story is often self-contained with no continuations. If you have confidence in being able to write short stories well, then give it a try. I'm not very good at short stories and don't have much confidence at improving to write short stories, but

don't let that stop you from having a crack at short stories – you might have more of a talent for it than I do.

Something to be wary of with your writing are taboos in relation to racism, sexism and portrayal of non-heterosexual characters, as being ignorant of these taboos could lead to one of your projects being considered controversial due to handling racism, sexism or sexuality poorly. Religion can be another subject where you should be mindful of taboos.

Other taboos to be mindful of are: portrayals of people with disabilities, regardless of whether the disability is physical or mental; mental illness, particularly being too flippant about it; etc.

To some extent, this applies to writers of both genders, but *especially* if you're a male writer, when writing female characters, try to avoid the following:

1. Ditzy characters who display a baffling lack of intelligence or even a lack of common sense
2. Oversexualised characters
3. Characters that are extremely shy and/or timid
4. Feminist man-haters, particularly ones who live in a supposedly utopian all-female society (unless you're satirising it)
5. Female characters who only function as a 'damsel in distress' role
6. Female characters who are only notable for being the wife or girlfriend of a male character, especially any who lack significant agency outside of such a

role (avoid such characters where possible and when appropriate)

When writing dialogue, conversations between two or more characters should change topic reasonably often like in real life rather than exhaustively discussing a single topic (which doesn't happen very often in real life). Try to have a logical progression of topics – where if you read the conversation from start to finish, you can see how one topic changed into the next, rather than randomly changing topic at a moment's notice. Also, a character being interrupted during conversation can be realistic, but try to avoid the interrupting character sounding unintentionally rude.

A good rule of thumb for an interrupting character would be to interrupt another character's monologuing – don't let a character launch into a multiple page monologue. If the character *must* have a monologue, have another character or an event interrupt their monologue – try to keep the monologuing character from continuing his/her monologue for more than one page. You can try to make the interruption humourous if you want.

Older RPGs (Role Playing Games) would usually have strict character limits for inputting character names e.g. 4 in Final Fantasy I, 5 in Final Fantasy V (five letter names), 6 in Final Fantasy IV, 7 (Final Fantasy VIII), 8 (FFX), 9 (Final Fantasy VIII GF's [Guardian Forces]), Ex-soldier (FFVII – 10, including the hyphen). Sources: FFI & II Dawn of Souls GBA remakes, Final Fantasy V (from memory), and Final Fantasy VII PS1 (FFVII PSN PS3), Final Fantasy VIII PS1 and PSN, Final Fantasy X HD Remaster (PS4 version).

Try experimenting with these different character limits for character names as a way to challenge yourself to write efficiently (though I'd recommend a character limit of at least 5 but preferably 6 – a four-character limit is extremely restrictive for character names and doesn't offer much flexibility).

Another writing exercise in a similar vein that would be useful for challenging yourself as a writer would be to practice writing Haiku – a form of Japanese poetry consisting of 3 lines of an alternating number of allowed syllables, with the intention being to challenge the writer to write well within the syllable limit and not write terrible poetry that sounds like gibberish (it's harder than you might think!). Alternatively, practise writing 'one-liners'.

Writing normal poetry would also be helpful, in English at least, rhyming is essential for poetry, but it won't have the syllable limit like haikus. Practicing normal poetry can lend itself to writing lyrics, although unless you're planning for your writing career to be purely as a lyricist, you probably won't be writing many lyrics.

I'd advise to generally disregard "write what you know" unless you're planning to write non-fiction, because if you followed 'write what you know' too closely and interpreted it in the wrong way, your creative work would be fairly autobiographical and fairly unimaginative. Instead, I suggest "write what you *want* (to)", keeping in mind the expression "art imitates life" – inspiration from real-life is fine, but try to be as imaginative as possible as often as possible.

If you're planning on creating a constructed mythology (conmyth) for a project or franchise, make sure that your conmyth is well-thought-out and that every aspect of your conmyth is created thoughtfully and create any original mythical beings sparingly. For any original mythical beings that you do create, make them distinct and unique and not too similar to any existing mythical being (e.g. don't just create a horse-like mythical being whose only major difference from a unicorn or Pegasus is an extra tail or an extra head).

Recently, I made some major tweaks to some constructed mythology I wasn't satisfied with – I tweaked some names for beings in the mythos called the Lords of Heaven and changed them from angel names to an assortment of Latin and Greek names, which I was much more satisfied with. I have a franchise about angels, so the 'placeholder angel names' are able to be repurposed for the angel franchise where they are a much more natural fit. This is a potential mistake I hope readers avoid – I hope you're sure you know roughly what language(s) you're aiming for with your constructed mythology *before* you start working on it.

If you'd prefer to stick with existing mythology (fairies, angels, pagan gods, etc), there's a lot of flexibility, but be prepared to research that mythology thoroughly, not just on the internet, but also non-fiction books. In this modern world, there should be virtually no excuse for mythology-based works that are poorly researched since it's easy to do internet searches, read Wikipedia articles, find non-fiction mythology books, etc. The only excuses I would consider acceptable for lack of research should be:

1. Lack of internet access (if due to poverty, natural disaster, or fire)

2. Non-fiction books about the chosen mythology being out of print or unavailable second-hand through any online retailers
3. You haven't made a final decision about which mythology your work will be based on

Laziness is not an acceptable excuse for not researching the chosen mythology thoroughly as what it suggests about you as a writer is that:

1. You don't take the chosen mythology seriously enough and aren't prepared to do the mythos justice or respect the source material
2. You're more interested in getting your name out there and getting paid than developing a reputation for excellent writing
3. You don't have enough respect for people who have an interest in mythology

Mythology (such as fairies, angels, pagan gods, etc) is essentially Public Domain unless you wrote something so similar to an existing franchise that it could be confused with it, or there was original conmyth from another creative work used in any of your mythology-based projects without permission from the copyright holder for that conmyth. Generally, as long as your mythology-based project(s) or franchise(s) are an original interpretation of the mythology, it's unlikely that you'll be sued for copyright infringement. Regardless of your chosen mythology, try to avoid simply retelling the original myths without at least putting twists on them or giving them comedic interpretations. Keep in mind the List of Mythologies article on Wikipedia for researching mythology.

Consider choosing an under-represented mythology, and avoid Japanese mythology (unless you're actually Japanese) as the Japanese are far more familiar with the mythos, many Japanese video games and anime already feature Japanese mythology, and because the Japanese can be insular in relation to creative works from the West (as in not paying much attention to or showing much interest in them) – a Westernised interpretation of Japanese mythology might not get released in Japan and if it does, would likely be relatively unsuccessful (but not always, as the success of video game Ghost of Tsushima proves, though it was a collaboration between a Western developer and the Japanese which probably helped it succeed in Japan).

If you're Japanese and reading this, I apologise if this causes offense, but I'd caution against writing projects that have either 1. Western demon lore and mythos or   2. angels as a significant amount of research is necessary to do those subjects justice, and Western demon lore and mythos generally requires familiarity with Christianity and books like the Bible, Paradise Lost, and The Divine Comedy as a starting point, not to mention further

research from books such as The Book of Enoch, The Book of Jubilees, various grimoires, in addition to a Biblical Hebrew dictionary and Modern Hebrew dictionary (for a series about angels), which can put a Japanese writer at a disadvantage with 1. and 2. compared to a Western writer where 1. and 2. can be major strengths of Western writers.

If you plan to write angel fiction, consider *both* a Biblical

Hebrew dictionary and Modern Hebrew dictionary the bare minimum amount of research for writing angel fiction – no offense, but if you're not prepared to do even *that* amount of research about angels and that relatively modest financial investment in your writing, you probably shouldn't be writing angel fiction.

Remember that angel names usually end in -el, but some don't. Speaking of 'don't', don't give your angel characters entirely human-sounding names, unless they have an urgent need to conceal their angelic identity (some angel characters would find that easier to do than others, depending on their name).

If you're a Japanese reader of this book, I'd highly recommend choosing a subject you'd likely to be fairly familiar with or at least more acquainted with than Christianity, such as Japanese mythology, Buddhism, Chinese mythology, Hinduism, and Hindu mythology. I would also suggest choosing something like Celtic mythology, Roman mythology, Greek mythology, Norse mythology or even Slavic mythology as an alternative to Western demonology or angels as they are much easier to research and lack of familiarity would be much less noticeable. You could even choose an obscure mythology like Native American mythology, Aztec mythology, Maori mythology, Gnosticism or even Australian Aboriginal mythology if you want to impress a Western audience. Even a manga, anime or video game series with a 'multiverse' of beings from multiple mythologies will still be easier than angels and require far less research!

If you're planning to go the conmyth route or otherwise planning to have a franchise about demons or involving demons in any significant way, consider using names for demons that start with or contain dae/dá/dé/dei (all pronounced 'day') to make their names sound demonic – this demonic association comes from the Zoroastrian Daeva, which were demons in Zoroastrianism tradition. Interestingly, it contrasts with Deva (pronounced the same as Daeva) in Hinduism where Devas are benevolent beings.

In the event you decide to have a franchise about or involving demons, have a go at inventing your own constructed demonology. Try choosing names from a variety of languages if you want to challenge yourself, and choosing a language/culture with insubstantial demonology to challenge yourself further – a language/culture such as English, especially if you're English speaking. Your invented demonology and/or portrayal of demons can be humourous if you want it to be.

If you have cultures based on particular real-life cultures, make sure that names of characters, towns, etc for those cultures are linguistically consistent with that real-world culture and that you make the decision to base your project's cultures on real-life cultures as early as possible. I had town names on hand-drawn maps, which I initially believed were gibberish and decided later (around 2010/2011) what real-life cultures the cultures in my work were based on. Some town names were able to be retro-actively translated to the respective cultures, but others didn't quite fit those languages. The names that didn't quite fit those languages I kept anyway because I sort of liked them and hadn't come up with any 'linguistically correct' town names to replace them.

I also have constructed languages (conlangs), and because some of the cultures were based on real-life cultures, most of my conlangs (constructed languages) are essentially fictional hybrids of real languages (an Irish and Gaelic hybrid, a Greek and Latin hybrid, a Ukrainian and Russian hybrid, and a blend of German, Swedish and Icelandic). In a sequel series, there are other constructed languages, but some are extremely underdeveloped, especially a nearly unused hybrid language and another language which is intended to sound demonic.

My most developed and original constructed language is Fae Spraesh, which draws influence mostly from Greek, Irish and Hebrew and is spoken by a culture that considers spirituality important – many spiritual or existential words in Fae Spraesh start with 'th-', and there are some words and phrases relating to spirituality that are virtually untranslatable, such as 'thae' – which loosely translates to mean 'anything of spiritual truth or reality', and also 'thaespraesh' – which loosely translates to 'conversation about spiritual topics'. Fae Spraesh is also intended to sound more beautiful when sung than English, reflecting its importance to that culture's spirituality.

My constructed languages are not incorporated into dialogue as much as I might like, but there are actual constructed languages for some of the cultures and it's possible to figure out roughly what real-life cultures they're based on (which is not to imply that every culture is based on a real-life culture, there definitely *are* alien races!).

You don't necessarily have to create any constructed languages yourself, but it adds believability to a setting whether the project is Sci-Fi or Fantasy. Keep in mind:
1. that creating constructed languages can be a massive undertaking
2. that to incorporate constructed languages into dialogue would require anywhere from 100-500 word (or more) constructed languages
3. that constructed languages are essentially never 'finished' unless they have about 50,000 words

If you're a Japanese writer, give creating constructed languages a reasonable amount of consideration, constructed languages aren't something I see from the Japanese all that often other than substitution ciphers (Al Bhed from Final Fantasy X was only a substitution cipher) – and if you're basing a culture in one of your projects on a culture from the West, consider constructed languages based on any of the following languages: Irish, Gaelic, Welsh, Greek, Russian, Ukrainian, German, Dutch, Swedish, Danish, Norwegian, Icelandic, French, Latin, Italian, Spanish, Portuguese, Hebrew.

For advice about constructed languages, see the *Writing Tips* chapter, and also my constructed language-related posts on my creative writing blog, zheretblog.wordpress.com. My blog is in English, so if you're not an English speaker, you might have to use webpage translation which I can't vouch for the accuracy of.

Before you start writing any scripts, make sure you're using a professional script writing program (such as Celtx or Final Draft). Generally avoid camera directions unless you need a very specific camera view such as First Person Perspective (or 'POV' [Point of View]), and generally avoid scene transitions unless you have a good understanding of creative works that used specific types of transitions effectively. The only camera directions you should use are PAN, ZAP TO (where the camera instantly moves to a particular location), ZOOM IN/OUT (generally on a location or object) or CLOSE UP (generally on a character), let a cinematographer figure out the rest of the camera directions.

If you can find any way of using perspectives like TOP DOWN or BOTTOM UP (Bottom Up being the opposite camera angle from Top Down) to great effect, then feel free to use them sparingly, but you probably won't need them particularly often.

Sometimes FADE TO BLACK can be used for dramatic effect. There is also FADE TO WHITE, but it's not as common. FADE TO in any colours other than black or white are fairly rare from my observations. FADE TO RED might be used in some situations to convey blood, but it's unlikely to be something you'll ever use. FADE TO BLACK/FADE TO WHITE should usually be written before the scene number/ scene location of the following scene, unless the FADE TO happens *during* a scene instead of at the beginning or end of a scene.

Some situations where FADE TO BLACK might be appropriate would be: a character is rendered unconscious (especially if by a villain), a character or multiple characters fall asleep, a character receives an injury that slowly causes them to become unconscious, to signify a significant amount of time has passed, etc. Some situations where FADE TO WHITE might be appropriate would be: a character begins a dream sequence, a character or multiple characters enter a place with extremely bright light, a character begins to hallucinate, etc. There may be other situations where either FADE TO BLACK or FADE TO WHITE might be appropriate or useful, the preceding two sentences aren't exhaustive. For example, for a character being rendered unconscious by a villain and then waking up in a different location, you might write FADE TO BLACK after whatever it was the villain did to render the character unconscious, then the scene number and scene location then simply write the next scene with the character waking up – POINT OF VIEW could be used if the character's vision is blurry when they wake up.

A similar technique is an IRIS SHOT (where a circle appears in the centre of the screen, generally surrounded by black, and the circle either expands or shrinks). Creative works that use this technique typically use it at the end of a creative work such as a TV show episode or movie.

If you have a dream sequence or flashback, type DREAM SEQUENCE or FLASHBACK into your script writing program at the beginning of the dream sequence or flashback and END DREAM SEQUENCE or END FLASHBACK at the end of the dream sequence or flashback. Slow motion is something you can use occasionally for dramatic or even humourous effect – type SLOW MOTION into your script and END SLOW MOTION when the slow motion is finished.

If you have one or more scenes where a character imagines a series of events that take place entirely within their imagination and in-universe never happen(ed), type IMAGINATION SEQUENCE into your script writing program at the beginning of the imaginary series of events and END IMAGINATION SEQUENCE at the end of the imaginary series of events.

The rule of thumb in relation to how page count relates to screen time is 1 page = 1 minute. For a 'half hour' TV show, aim for about 20-21 pages per script divided into three acts, for an 'hour long show', aim for about 40-42 pages. A video game script's length can vary greatly depending on genre and complexity of the narrative, particularly if Choice and Consequence have a significant presence in the game (Choice and Consequence will be discussed further later).

The biggest difference between 'half hour TV shows' and 'hour long TV shows', from a writing perspective, is that a show with 40-minute episodes will tend to have a lot more standalone episodes with self-contained stories and be less focused on a single, continuous narrative. Anime tends to be almost exclusively in the 20-minute episode range, and anime will generally have an ongoing plot and relatively few standalone episodes, except possibly some filler episodes. 40-minute shows will occasionally have 2-parters and sometimes even 3-parters.

Expect, or at least *allocate,* up to 1 week to write a half hour series script (especially if it's a comedic series), perhaps 2-3 weeks to write an hour-long series script (though none of my projects are hour long shows, so the 2-3 weeks figure is a guess), and maybe 6 weeks to write a movie script. For a novel, assume about 1 year, maybe 2 years, and for a video game script, anywhere from 6 months to a year (if it's an RPG) or anywhere between 1 and 6 months (perhaps 3-4 months) for most non-RPG genre video game scripts. These figures don't include tweaks and revisions, so don't forget to factor in and allocate time for those – these completion time figures are for the *first draft*.

If you're writing a video game script, when transitioning between gameplay and a cutscene, type CUTSCENE at the start of the cutscene and END CUTSCENE at the end of the cutscene. If there is interactivity in the cutscene such as dialogue options, these go BEFORE where you write END CUTSCENE. Write a list of all the dialogue options in that cutscene, then for each dialogue option, write "Player selects [insert dialogue option here])", then whatever dialogue or action(s) that result from that dialogue option. What triggers a particular cutscene to start – is it 'Player speaks to [insert character name]'?, 'Player enters/leaves [insert name of location]', 'Player approaches [insert name of location, character, object]' (or even 'Player activates [insert name of object or device]')?

Regarding optional cutscenes in video games (cutscenes the player is not required to see to advance the main plot), if a cutscene can be missed, for example, if a particular side quest wasn't completed before a certain point in the main plot, refer to such cutscenes in your video game script as a MISSABLE CUTSCENE.

If you have something like the player entering a room and all of the entrances and exits being sealed and the room filling with enemies where the player has to defeat all of the enemies before a cutscene plays, write PLAYER ENTERS (Insert name of room/location) then either CUTSCENE then describe the entrances and exits being sealed and the room filling with enemies, or alternatively, write it as an interactive cutscene (discussed later in this chapter) where the

events happen with the player still in control of the character. Then, to describe the player needing to defeat all the enemies in the room to proceed, write

PLAYER DEFEATS ALL ENEMIES, then write the cutscene that follows the defeat of the last enemy in the room (if there is one) or skip ahead in the script to the location of the next cutscene if defeating all of the enemies only unlocks entrances or exits.

Generally, a script should start with 'FADE IN', unless you're going for a COLD OPEN in which case the FADE IN is placed later, and at the end, FADE OUT. TITLE DROP (where the name and logo of the creative work/franchise appears on screen) is something you should use sparingly in a script, usually either with the proper FADE IN after having a COLD OPEN (or at the end of a prologue in a video game script), or at the end of a script just before FADE OUT.

If the game has the player obtaining an ability, piece of equipment, or key item (or in some rare cases, a consumable item) that has a particular function (typically non-combat) when it's used, write PLAYER OBTAINS (insert name of ability, equipment, key item), and if a tutorial is required to explain how to use that ability or piece of equipment, simply write TUTORIAL: (insert name of ability, piece of equipment, key item). The tutorial can be either during a cutscene or after a cutscene, I'll leave that decision to *you*.

When writing boss battles, which are relevant to multiple/most video game genres, write BOSS FIGHT: (insert name of boss) or BOSS BATTLE: (insert name of boss) and write (without the quotation marks) "(insert name of boss) is defeated:" before writing any cutscenes after the boss battle.

For cutscenes *during* a boss battle (which would be most likely in an RPG), write IN-BATTLE CUTSCENE and END IN-BATTLE CUTSCENE when it's finished. For a different phase of a boss battle (not necessarily a final boss), you'd write (without the quotation marks) "(insert name of boss) reaches (insert percentage or fraction) health:" then simply write a cutscene as usual.

If you're planning to write a video game script for any genre other than RPG (Role Playing Game), try to write cutscenes that are 5 pages or less – at the very least, don't make the mistake of writing cutscenes that are 10 pages or more in anything that's not in the RPG genre – doing so will peg you as an amateur writer. Metal Gear Solid 4 had a series of uninterrupted cutscenes that totalled 71 minutes – if you're Hideo Kojima or another highly regarded and well-established video game writer, you might get away with it, but if you're writing your first ever video game script (hopefully once you have 10 years of total writing experience), you'll want to keep most cutscenes 5 pages or less each (you might be able to make an exception for the ending, though).

Also, avoid 'cheating' with the length of cutscenes by having more than one cutscene without at least a short section of gameplay separating cutscenes, even something as simple as the player entering a building in the game, having one cutscene, the player leaving the building, then having another *short* cutscene. Without a section of gameplay separating two cutscenes, two '5-page cutscenes' would, in effect, be 10 minutes of cutscenes from the player's perspective. If you want, you can make an exception to the '5-page cutscene' rule for the ending, and have up to 10 pages for the ending.

RPGs are much more forgiving than most video game genres when it comes to long cutscenes, but if you're up for the challenge, try to write an RPG script where essentially every cutscene except maybe the ending, is 5 pages or less.

If you've ever noticed in a video game a scene where the main character and any other characters are walking or running and there's dialogue between them, but it seems like regular gameplay rather than a cutscene, I assume you'd write it as an interactive cutscene and just write the dialogue for that section of gameplay. I don't really have experience at writing that style of cutscene, but it's something you might want to consider as it can feel like gameplay rather than seem like a cutscene that doesn't have interactivity, and the' cutscene' blends naturally with the gameplay. Try writing INTERACTIVE CUTSCENE and END INTERACTIVE CUTSCENE, and specifying in your video game script the location the player needs to enter or action(s) the player needs to perform to start the cutscene as well as mentioning

anything that ends the cutscene prematurely (such as

opening a door that leads to a new location, picking up or interacting with a particular object, talking to a particular character, etc).

Try to use extended flashbacks sparingly in video game scripts, and if a particularly long flashback is required for plot reasons or is necessary for character development, at least try making the non-cutscene parts of the flashback interactive. You can start the interactive flashback with INTERACTIVE FLASHBACK, with cutscenes within the flashback written in the ordinary way (CUTSCENE at the start, END CUTSCENE at the end) and END INTERACTIVE FLASHBACK when the interactive flashback is finished.

If you're planning to write a video game script, you might decide you want the game to have a significant amount of Choice and Consequence (decisions and/or dialogue options that affect the plot, outcome of side quests, etc) – writing Choice and Consequence in a video game is a fairly advanced skill, and it's better to tackle it when you already have experience with it, or can find someone who does have experience at writing Choice and Consequence in video game scripts who'd be willing to mentor you. Trying to tackle Choice and Consequence when you're an inexperienced writer would be a waste of time as the quality is unlikely to be your best work.

Also, you risk overreaching and potentially embarrassing yourself as a writer by revealing yourself to be out of your depth.

If you're especially keen on tackling Choice and Consequence, especially if RPGs are your desired genre, try practicing by writing at least one regular RPG script that has no or minimal use of Choice and Consequence first, then transition to significant use of Choice and Consequence when you feel confident enough. Remember, try to have a minimum of 5 years of total writing experience before attempting a video game script, preferably 10 when you'll have greater experience, confidence and a certain level of maturity as a writer.

Multiple endings is something that usually only works in video games due to games being interactive. The classic Super Nintendo RPG Chrono Trigger had 12 endings (13 in rerelease versions) in addition to the 'bad' ending, but wisely, the developer chose to never make a direct sequel to avoid upsetting players who favoured a specific ending. You'll probably want to have 5 or less endings, and for each ending to be significantly different than the others.

Some video games have a 'bad' ending, which is often the default ending, and will have a 'true' ending that requires specific steps to unlock. The complexity of unlocking the 'true' ending depends on the game – some video games' 'true' endings are relatively easy to unlock, while some games will have a long checklist of requirements to unlock it, where missing even a single requirement prevents the player from unlocking the 'true' ending. In rarer situations, a game will make the 'bad' ending extremely hard to unlock where the player has to go out of their way to get the 'bad' ending. If you end up working with a game developer, the endings might be something worth discussing with them, including the steps necessary to unlock the 'true' ending (assuming your game has more than one ending).

Further writing advice can be found in the *Writing Tips* chapter.

Contemplating Comedy

You don't need to be a stand-up comedian or have stand-up experience to write comedic work (but I assume it does help), but if you notice that a project lends itself to comedy, don't hold back! Keep in mind that even if you have talent at writing comedy, it doesn't automatically mean you'd be suited to being a stand-up comedian.

There are different styles of comedy, such as puns, literal interpretation, satire, parodies, exaggeration, running jokes, etc. Each style is useful, but avoid being over-reliant on puns for humour – the best humour from puns often comes from characters making references to it, especially if it's a terrible pun where it becomes a running joke with characters making references to how terrible the pun is.

A running joke should evolve and mutate the longer it stays in use, such that it gets treated as a meme within the context of the creative work it appears in – don't just recycle the original joke.

Literal interpretation is where a particular word or expression is interpreted literally instead of figuratively. The more unusual, weird or illogical a particular expression is, the more likely it might be to lend itself to humour.

There can be a degree of overlap between satire and parodies, particularly if something is described as a 'satirical parody', but in legal contexts, some of the freedom of expression laws that protect parodies are not necessarily extended to satire, but you shouldn't worry about lawsuits due to satire unless it contains defamation. However, defamation generally requires proof of ill intent and usually contains slander and libel – comedy is usually written (or at least *should* be written) without ill intent.

Try to avoid 'slapstick' humour – even though not much is lost in translation between languages with slapstick humour, it's not particularly clever humour and generally involves physical injuries and accidents being played for laughs.

'Brevity is the soul of wit' (Hamlet, Act 2, Scene 2) is an important thing to keep in mind with writing generally, but especially when it comes to comedy. Long-winded monologues and speeches are something to avoid, and especially long-winded jokes that use dialogue inefficiently should be avoided as much as possible. You demonstrate your talent for writing more by writing succinctly rather than verbosely (being excessively wordy) – think 'quality, not quantity'; 'less is more'.

Never write prolonged jokes that are half a page, let alone longer, before they get to the humorous part (which might not have enough of a payoff to be worth such a long setup), in half a page, particularly with a machine gun comedy approach, you could have 2-3 jokes (or possibly even more) just in that half a page setup that were each funnier than the half a page or longer single joke. That's especially true if the payoff for the half a page or longer single joke was just a mildly humourous pun. Machine gun comedy needs to be succinct and punchy – it's about economy of words, writing more *efficiently* rather than just 'writing *more*'.

Avoid writing comedic scripts that go multiple pages without any laugh out loud moments – if you have any comedic scripts that go for 3 or more pages without anything that makes you, the writer, laugh out loud, that's a sign those scripts are in serious need of tweaking. The world doesn't need comedies that fail to *get* the audience laughing, let alone *keep* them laughing.

When writing comedic scripts, aim for a minimalist plot – this doesn't mean a 'bad' plot, just a simple one. A minimalist plot should not be completely impossible in real-life unless there are fantasy/mythology/supernatural elements, or be totally nonsense (unless the intention is to make the plot's absurdity a running joke) but should take up as little screen time as possible. If you want to write detailed, complex storylines, if you're writing comedy, you're looking at the wrong genre.

If you start to develop a talent for writing decent or at least passable haikus, then you'll be able to write dialogue more efficiently, and just as importantly, when you've finished a script, you'll be able to work within the number of words and sentences of the existing dialogue when 'tweaking' scripts. This can be essential to writing comedic projects, as you'll learn how to replace any flat or unimportant dialogue (i.e. any dialogue that's not essential for plot or character development) with succinct humour using roughly the same number of words and sentences.

When you have a completed script to work with (or at least a completed first draft), you're then able to tweak the dialogue to your heart's content. Writing comedic projects at the 'tweaked' level of quality on a first draft – now *that* is something that will take a lot of talent!

For comedic scripts, don't just assume the completed first draft is the final version, let alone assume that script is the highest quality it can be and can't improve in any way – you might find some of your earlier comedic scripts weren't quite as good as you thought they were at the time. Depending on how long you've been writing comedic scripts (if you *have* been), there may be a noticeable difference between your most recent comedic scripts and your earliest ones.

If a comedic script can still benefit from tweaking, then go ahead and tweak it! What you should be on the lookout for in those first drafts are any sections of 'flat' dialogue – basically any dialogue that's not essential for plot or character development or that doesn't already have something humourous. When you've tweaked dialogue to make it funnier to such an extent that you'd be interfering with dialogue related to the plot if you tried tweaking dialogue any further, then that script might be ready. Try not to think of or approach tweaking scripts as (figuratively) taking a hacksaw to your scripts, try to think of and approach it as bringing out the full potential of those scripts.

Of all areas of the creative industry, comedy is possibly scarcest in the video game industry – I know of very few franchises, let alone one-off games that were especially comedic. I doubt it's really as simple as there being a lack of comedians and comedy writers having transitioned into video game writing. I assume the main reason for the lack of comedy in video games is because game developers have decided that comedy loses some of its impact after the audience has heard a particular joke for the first time, and that after multiple playthroughs the impact of the comedy would continue to diminish since there's no 'surprise factor' with any of the jokes (although this also affects re-watching comedy on DVD/Blu-Ray or streaming).

If you want to try writing a comedic video game script, be absolutely sure you have complete confidence in your ability to write comedic content. Make sure that comedy is a focus before you start writing that script so that comedy is there from the beginning, rather than being shoehorned into a non-comedic script as a last-minute decision.

I usually have fun when I'm writing comedic stuff (who wouldn't want to be able to laugh at something funny they wrote?), and the more enjoyment I get out of writing, the more I'll want to write. One of the reasons I have so much fun writing comedic content is because even though I'll have a small number of jokes pre-planned as a rough guide, the majority of the humour develops organically while I'm writing, and I'll often be genuinely surprised by how the humour evolves.

When I made the decision to write an ultra-low budget comedy movie (Larrikings), one of the reasons I chose to write an ultra-low budget movie was because the next lowest risk creative project I had was an 18-episode satirical series (which is a spin-off of a 49-episode series), which I had no success in getting any script reads of, let alone success in getting it produced even when I offered the option of producing the 18-episode series first as a 'low risk' option. I decided that an ultra-low budget movie would be taking away the majority of the risk of an original project by an unproduced writer and potentially would have much more success at getting script reads and hopefully, getting produced.

Unfortunately, I went through a list of 130 U.S screenwriting managers, and excluding any that had no website or no email address (or in some cases, neither), not a single screenwriting manager requested a script read for Larrikings even despite its ultra-low budget. Ironically, I got the most responses from ones that were listed as not accepting unsolicited queries, though they were the 'carefully worded PR response' kind of response where they had excuses for why they weren't able to read the script. Whether the fact that I was technically a 'foreign' writer (being based in Australia) was a factor on why none of the screenwriting managers requested a script read, I don't know.

Suffice to say I was pretty disappointed, as I had thought that with such a low-risk movie, at least a small number of screenwriting managers would have been interested in seeing if the script was humourous enough and worth producing, especially since I briefly summarised my creative portfolio including mentioning the books I'd written, but alas, even then they still weren't interested. I blame timewasters – I'm fairly convinced agents, screenwriting managers and producers probably ignore virtually all of their emails unless they come from someone they already know in the creative industry.

Some other reasons I chose comedy for my ultra-low budget movie were:

1. Because I usually have fun writing comedy, I'd have fun writing the ultra-low budget movie and it wouldn't be something I didn't believe in or wasn't passionate about.
2. Comedy can be done on an ultra-low budget without having to make too many sacrifices (Horror is the other genre that can work well on ultra-low budgets).
3. To challenge myself to see if I could make a comedy work with limited characters and limited locations.

If you don't feel confident in your ability to write comedy, please don't get the wrong idea and think I'm suggesting that you force yourself to write comedy – you can give it a go, but if you decide you're not very good at comedy, or you gave it your best for a while and didn't feel like your ability to write comedy improved by much or felt like you weren't able to make it work, don't force yourself.

If it's any consolation, I didn't foresee myself writing comedic content earlier on with my writing – it was in large part due to the influence of a High School friend that I considered comedic writing, and I only started writing comedic content seriously (as in, in a serious capacity, since obviously the point of comedy is that it's *not* serious) after about 8-9 years of writing, and gradually became more confident with it.

If you plan to write comedy, you could do a lot worse than watching every episode of Seinfeld and other highly-regarded comedy shows for research.

I hope some of you who read this book discover a latent talent for writing comedy and develop the confidence to 'get serious' about comedy. The world could certainly use more laughter, especially with the global COVID situation, since it's been said and often repeated that 'laughter is the best medicine' (as long as you don't interpret that literally – good luck curing COVID-19 with laughter!).

Japanese Creative Quirkiness

In this chapter, I'd like to discuss an aspect of Japanese creativity that I tend to refer to as 'Japanese Creative Quirkiness'. For parts of this chapter, Japanese Creative Quirkiness will be abbreviated to JCQ.

One aspect of Japanese Creative Quirkiness I've read about is a Japanese fascination with names they consider especially exotic. This can either work for them or against them, as I'm about to explain.

When JCQ works in favour of the Japanese, we can expect to see some interesting and possibly even *inspired* ideas (one example is the summon Alexander from the Final Fantasy series - based on presumably nothing other than the name Alexander the Great, they came up with a fortress-like robot that fires holy-element missiles [all *that* just from the name of Alexander the Great?], and the name translates to either 'leader of men' or 'defender of mankind' – to avoid spoilers, suffice to say the latter translation has significance in Final Fantasy IX), but when it works *against* them, there's what I refer to as the 'Tina-Terra situation' with Final Fantasy VI where they considered Tina an exotic name but discovered it was a common Western name so it was changed to Terra in the Western version [although, thankfully, it created a 'heaven and earth' parallel between Terra and Celes].

Still on the subject of the Final Fantasy series, there's also the summon Leviathan. In Christianity, Leviathan has some notoriety as a Biblical sea-demon, but the makers of the Final Fantasy series envisioned Leviathan as a benevolent water-element summon. A bold choice!

These are just not necessarily exhaustive examples from only a single Japanese creative franchise.

JCQ usually only works against the Japanese when they failed on a particular occasion to conduct research to see if a name was uncommon or rare in the West. Or, if the Japanese attempted Western demonology or angels (both topics a Western writer with knowledge of Christianity will generally be more familiar with), especially if not much research was involved.

In any case, be wary of randomness. An example of randomness would be the Final Fantasy VI Esper Bismarck, which takes the form of a giant whale. The name Bismarck comes from a World War II-era German warship, which in turn was named after a German emperor. The etymology of the name Bismarck has no connections whatsoever to whales (or even oceans), so presumably, the connection between that Esper and whales was the German warship named Bismarck. This presumably must have made sense to some of the staff who worked on Final Fantasy VI (or they would have chosen a different name for the Esper – 'Jonah' would have made more sense), but to Western audiences, it seems very 'random' (with the possible exception of Germans, who might have found it amusing).

If you're a Japanese writer and reading a translated version of this book, firstly, I hope I haven't offended you by cautioning against projects based on Western demonology or angels, and secondly, if you're planning to use names from the West, pay attention to the etymology of the names (what the names translate from in their original language) to avoid names that might sound pleasing to the ear but which translate into essentially gibberish that lacks any deeper meaning or worse still, are so silly as to be unintentionally humourous to Western audiences (which can be a problem if you were aiming for meaningful character names). Exceptions would be things like invented names that imitate an existing language but have no translation in that language, and invented names that are entirely original especially if they have a sufficiently exotic constructed language-like quality to them (a corresponding constructed language that those invented names originate from is *optional*, but the extra effort adds authenticity).

You don't need to worry too much about the meaning of a character's name for a character with a Western name (a character's full name doesn't necessarily have to have a meaningful translation), but do try to aim for believability – if character is intended to have a French, German, Italian, Spanish, Latin, Greek, or Slavic name (Slavic languages are numerous enough I chose not to include an exhaustive list), research names in those languages and create character names that could theoretically occur in those languages (even if only rarely), as opposed to names that only sound like one of those languages but are not actual words in those languages – that can undermine the believability of such character names. For towns with Western names, a meaningful translation is preferable to gibberish.

The Japanese are (at least, from my observations), the world-leader in the type of creativity I tend to call 'original creature design' (e.g. Pokémon, Digimon, Yokai Watch), and 'original creature design' is one of their greatest creative strengths. However, it's a difficult type of creativity to do well, as it helps to have a video game franchise to showcase the creatures, and the writing is far less important than the artwork of the creatures themselves.

Another aspect of JCQ I've discovered was the invented angel sub-ranks in the Bayonetta games - they were obviously familiar with the basic 9 Choir angelic hierarchy, and came up with a few ideas of their own. It's hard to say whether a Western writer would have come up with the same idea, it was kind of an 'out of left field' idea. There was also the manga Saint Young Men, where Jesus and Buddha returned to earth and were best friends.

If you're a Japanese writer, feel free to double-down on Japanese Creative Quirkiness and focus on less research-intensive subjects than Western demonology and angels such as

Shinto, Buddhism, and various mythologies, and let Western writers handle Western demonology and angels. This way, creativity is focused on creative strengths rather than two topics where Western writers are more knowledgeable (particularly due to familiarity with Christianity) and that creativity can be redirected to where it will best serve Japanese writers and achieve better creative outcomes. Likewise, it's only fair that as a sign of respect for the Japanese, Western writers should avoid writing creative works based on Japanese mythology. This advice is well-intentioned, as I, and many other Westerners, have deep respect for Japanese creativity (I personally am a big fan of Japanese RPGs [JRPGs] and anime), but nonetheless, I apologise if this advice has caused offense.

If you're a Japanese writer and you absolutely insist on writing creative works featuring Western demonology and/or angels, at least make every reasonable effort to thoroughly research the lore and mythos via Wikipedia articles, non-fiction books, etc, and make every reasonable effort to have at least a basic knowledge of Christianity (for example, familiarity with Bible passages mentioning demons or angels) as even Japanese Creative Quirkiness can have a hard time concealing lack of familiarity with the topics.

Also, if you're not only a Japanese writer, but plan to one day work for Atlus (the developer of the Megami Tensei franchise, which features a variety of mythological beings and from time to time, obscure demonology or angel mythos), thorough research of Western demonology and angel mythos would essentially be a prerequisite. You might instead consider an original franchise such as a manga about Western demonology or angels (I'd recommend choosing one or the other instead of both, so that your manga has more room to explore the topic you chose), but don't rush into it – try to have a strong grasp of the mythos before committing to such a manga, exhaust virtually every source of lore about Western demonology and/or angels that you can find, whether online or non-fiction books. Even if some non-fiction books about Western demonology or angels have no Japanese translation available, they may still be useful for cataloguing demon or angel names.

You don't need to be an expert on Christianity (Western audiences wouldn't have that expectation of Japanese writers), but if you're able to show familiarity with the Bible, and for extra credit, Paradise Lost, The Divine Comedy, the Book of Enoch, Book of Jubilees, etc, you might surprise Western audiences. If you choose to focus on demonology rather than angels, consider researching grimoires for listings of demons. If you feel empowered rather than discouraged, then I'm glad I was able to help you.

I'll keep my eye out for any other expressions of Japanese Creative Quirkiness, a reasonable amount of the time, it's interesting to see what the Japanese come up with. If you are a Japanese writer, I hope you've found this chapter informative and useful, especially if the concept of Japanese Creativity Quirkiness was something you may have been unaware of or hadn't thought much about before reading this chapter.

Keep up the creative quirkiness, Japan, it's part of what the West admires about your creativity! Write on!

Creative Affirmations

In this chapter I've included creative affirmations. Recite these affirmations, and say 'yes' after each one. The purpose of these affirmations is not necessarily to draw creative opportunities to you (there *is* a concept in spirituality known as the Law of Attraction, but affirmations haven't led to creative opportunities for me yet), but to give you confidence as a writer. When many or even most of these affirmations feel authentic for you as a writer, you'll have confidence in your writing ability, and experience and confidence are two of the most important assets for a writer.

Be mindful of 'creative blockages', and be extremely mindful of any 'I will never…' statements, such as 'I will never be as good a writer as [insert writer's name here]', 'I will never catch up to [insert writer's name here]' and anything self-defeating, statements like 'I will never get anything produced' or 'I will never get [insert name of project] produced'.

Besides creative jealousy when comparing yourself to other writers, you're creating an expectation of failure and might subconsciously sabotage your writing. Also, it might make you fall into the habit of criticising your own work far too harshly because you've set an imaginary writing quality standard that you don't think you'll ever be able to reach. It might even be possible that you've overvalued a particular writer's work, and when seen more objectively, it might still be high quality, even excellent, but not as untouchable as you imagined.

In the earlier years of my creative writing, I idolised the Final Fantasy writers and put them on a pedestal because I was so amazed by the Final Fantasy games I'd played growing up. I later learned that Final Fantasy X's script was written in only 3 and a half months, and when I played through Final Fantasy X the second time via the HD collection, I noticed much of the dialogue was less eloquent than I remembered and sometimes sections of dialogue were repeated in such a way that it seemed like a character was stuttering. Needless to say, my opinion of the Final Fantasy writers changed a bit after that and I stopped thinking of them as untouchable. The Final Fantasy series was a major creative influence, at least, and is probably still my greatest creative influence and I'm grateful for not only the creative influence the Final Fantasy series provided, but also the entertainment the games provided me.

This will probably sound quite 'out there', but in Theta Healing, I did get tested for creative blockages related to the Final Fantasy series and Final Fantasy writers, and some of them, including 'I will never…' statements were there, so I had those creative blockages cleared in Theta.

Feelings of inferiority and inadequacy towards other writers are generally bad, especially in relation to your confidence and ability to assess things such as your own writing or other writers' writing objectively. Once you have 10 years or more of writing experience, especially if you've been making many creative breakthroughs along the way, try to avoid the opposite extreme of getting too arrogant about your writing such that *you* end up being the one you think is untouchable. If you're too cocky about your writing you'll probably be unable to accept criticism, possibly not even constructive criticism and may end up developing a reputation of being a writer who is considered too difficult to work with. Be confident yet humble!

Without further ado (since there's already been so *much* ado), here are the creative affirmations:

"On all levels, creativity and spirituality exist
in harmony and complement each other."

"On all levels, I am successful in
all that I set my mind to."

"On all levels, I am worthy of being creative."

"On all levels, I am worthy of
receiving divine inspiration."

"On all levels, it is my right to be creative."

"On all levels, all creative goals I set for
myself can and will be achieved."

"On all levels, I create success as a writer."

"On all levels, my writing is excellent quality."

"On all levels, my creative projects are meaningful."

"On all levels, creativity is meaningful."

"On all levels, my creative projects are recognised."

"On all levels, my creative projects are successful."

"On all levels, I am respected as a writer."

"On all levels, I am acknowledged as a writer."

"On all levels, my creative projects are accepted."

"On all levels, my writing is worthy of recognition and praise."

"On all levels, I am worthy of recognition and acceptance."

"On all levels, creativity is my joy."

"On all levels, creativity is my gift."

"On all levels, creativity is service to myself and others."

"On all levels, creativity is power."

"On all levels, creativity is wisdom."

"On all levels, my creativity, in any and all creative mediums I choose to work in and with, including: novels, television series – including animation, video games, web series, graphic novels, and lyrics, as well as any unspecified internet-based media, is *always* wanted, accepted, appreciated, recognised, respected and acknowledged."

"On all levels, my creativity, in any and all creative mediums I choose to work in and with, including: novels, television series – including animation, video games, web series, graphic novels, and lyrics, as well as any unspecified internet-based media, is *always* wanted, accepted, appreciated, recognised, respected and acknowledged by the Universe and the Creator."

"On all levels, creativity leads me to honour the Creator, serve the Creator, praise the Creator, develop gratitude for the Creator's blessings, and allows me to experience self-love, self-confidence and spiritual growth."

"On all levels, brilliant and original creative ideas come to me naturally."

"On all levels, the Creator has ambitious plans for my creativity."

"On all levels, I now claim unlimited creative opportunities for myself."

"On all levels, my creative vision is capable of receiving unlimited divine inspiration."

"On all levels, when I take risks creatively, they usually pay off."

"On all levels, I trust my creative process."

"On all levels, I have an abundance of writing talent."

"On all levels, my creativity continues to evolve and I continue to grow as a writer."

Creative Projects-specific:

"On all levels, my creative projects deserve to be produced without exception and the Creator intends this for me."

"On all levels, my creative projects deserve commercial success."

"On all levels, my creative projects deserve to be acknowledged by producers, directors and creative company CEOs within the creative industry."

"On all levels, my creative projects are able to be produced in this dimension without exception."

"On all levels, I deserve to receive interest in a creative project when I email a producer."

"On all levels, my creative projects deserve
to receive interest from a producer."

"On all levels, my creative projects
will be produced, and will now
enter production promptly."

"On all levels, my creative projects
deserve to be discovered by producers,
directors and creative company CEOs
and the Creator intends this for me."

"On all levels, I am being discovered as a writer by
producers, directors and creative company CEOs."

"On all levels, I am well-suited as a
writer for all creative situations."

"On all levels, everything creative I
touch and work on is a success."

"On all levels, I am deeply fulfilled by
all that I do with creative writing."

"On all levels, creative opportunities are abundant,
and my creativity prospers in every way."

"On all levels, I have a promising
future as a writer, full of fulfilment and
amazing creative achievements."

"On all levels, my creative work and creative
projects are recognised, respected, accepted,

appreciated and acknowledged by producers."

"On all levels, my creative work and creative projects are recognised, respected, accepted, appreciated and acknowledged by everyone in the creative industry."

"On all levels, the Creator intends for me to be successful as a writer."

"On all levels, the Creator intends for me to succeed commercially, artistically and spiritually with creative works."

"On all levels, I am established enough as a writer to satisfy a producer."

"On all levels, I am established enough as a writer to satisfy a producer to produce one of my creative projects."

"On all levels, creativity is a meaningful use of time."/ "On all levels, my creativity is a meaningful use of time."

"On all levels, creativity is rewarding."/ "On all levels, my creativity is rewarding."

"On all levels, creativity is fulfilling."/ "On all levels, my creativity is fulfilling."

"On all levels, creativity creates financial abundance."/ "On all levels, my creativity creates financial abundance."

"On all levels, my creativity brings me financial abundance."

"On all levels, my creative writing brings me financial abundance."

"On all levels, my creative projects bring me financial abundance."

"On all levels, creativity is spiritually rewarding."/ "On all levels, my creativity is spiritually rewarding."

"On all levels, creativity is financially rewarding."/ "On all levels, my creativity is financially rewarding."

"On all levels, creativity is artistically rewarding."/ "On all levels, my creativity is artistically rewarding."

"On all levels, creativity is vocationally rewarding."/ "On all levels, my creativity is vocationally rewarding."

"On all levels, creativity is immensely spiritually, financially, artistically and vocationally rewarding."/ "On all levels, my creativity is immensely spiritually, financially, artistically and vocationally rewarding."

"On all levels, my creative talent is recognised, respected, accepted, appreciated and acknowledged by producers."

"On all levels, my creative talent is recognised, respected, accepted, appreciated and acknowledged by everyone in the creative industry."

"On all levels, it is possible to be creative in this world and do so with ease and grace."

"On all levels, it is possible to be creative in Australia and do so with ease and grace."

"On all levels, it is both possible and easy to receive a response when I email a producer."

"On all levels, it is both possible and easy to receive interest in a creative project when I email a producer."

"On all levels, it is possible to have creative projects produced in this world, have them be commercially successful, and do so with ease and grace."

"On all levels, I am a remarkable writer."

"On all levels, anything is possible with my creative projects and franchises."

"On all levels, only I decide what is impossible for me as a writer."

"On all levels, I am growing in confidence, skill, and experience as a writer."

"On all levels, I am the creator of my destiny."

"On all levels, my creative writing efforts are admirable."

"On all levels, I have deep faith in my own creative talents."

"On all levels, my creative works can create positive change."

"On all levels, there are endless possibilities for my creativity."

"On all levels, only I set the limits of my creativity."

"On all levels, I can be as creative as I choose to be."

Creative Affirmations (Success, Manifest/Attract, Agent related):

"On all levels, I easily and readily manifest all creative opportunities that I require."

"On all levels, my creative projects always attract abundant interest from producers."

"On all levels, producers always want

to read one or more or my scripts."

"On all levels, producers always offer to read a script when I email them."

"On all levels, I am always highly sought after as a writer by producers."

"On all levels, my creative projects are always highly sought after by producers."

"On all levels, producers are eager to produce my creative projects."

"On all levels, my creative projects have irresistible appeal and producers are eager to produce them."

"On all levels, agents in the creative industry are interested in representing me."

"On all levels, agents in the creative industry appreciate my creative projects."

"On all levels, agents in the creative industry are eager to represent me."

"On all levels, it is easy to secure an agent in the creative industry to represent me."

"On all levels, abundant spiritual, artistic, critical, commercial and financial success are attracted to all that I do with creative projects."

"On all levels, abundant spiritual, artistic, critical,

Creative Affirmations

commercial and financial success are attracted to each and every of my creative projects."

"On all levels, everyone in the creative industry that I work with finds me to be a joy and a pleasure to work with."

"On all levels, producers in the creative industry are eager to peruse my creative projects."

"On all levels, my creative projects receive instant acclaim whenever a script is read by a producer or agent in the creative industry and whenever one of my creative projects is produced."

"On all levels, producers and agents in the creative industry are receptive and attentive to me as a writer."

"On all levels, my creative projects are an instant success whenever one of them is produced."

"On all levels, producers and agents in the creative industry have complete faith in my potential and creative talent."

"On all levels, I am in the correct nation for what I want to achieve with creativity."

"On all levels, I am fully ready to receive all creative opportunities I require."

"On all levels, I always attract all the creative

opportunities I require whenever I need them."

"On all levels, producers, screenwriting managers and agents in the creative industry easily recognise and appreciate my innovative ideas."

"On all levels, producers, screenwriting managers and agents in the creative industry recognise and appreciate my unique voice and perspective as a writer."

"On all levels, my unique voice and perspective as a writer are widely recognised and appreciated within the creative industry."

"On all levels, my creative writing entertains and inspires joy in all producers, screenwriting managers and agents in the creative industry who read it."

"On all levels, producers, screenwriting managers and agents in the creative industry are enthusiastic about reading my scripts."

'Writing Career' Affirmations

"On all levels, my career as a writer/my writing career [try both] abounds with critical acclaim, financial abundance, abundant career opportunities, and unlimited potential."

"On all levels, my writing career is continually reaching greater career opportunities, greater recognition and greater realisation of all kinds."

"On all levels, my writing career, in terms of career opportunities, recognition, and critical acclaim, is rapidly gaining momentum."

"On all levels, my writing career is extremely successful and I attract respect, praise and career opportunities with every project I devote my time and effort to."

"On all levels, producers immediately recognise my creative talent and potential."

"On all levels, agents in the creative industry immediately recognise my creative talent and potential."

"On all levels, everyone in the creative industry immediately recognises my creative talent and potential."

"On all levels, producers immediately recognise the value and potential of my creative projects."

"On all levels, agents in the creative industry immediately recognise the value and potential of my creative projects."

"On all levels, everyone in the creative

industry immediately recognises the value and potential of my creative projects."

"On all levels, every creative project I conceive of, without exception, can be produced in this dimension."

"On all levels, every creative goal I set for myself can be achieved in this dimension."

"On all levels, producers reply promptly and courteously when I email them."

"On all levels, screenwriting managers in the creative industry reply promptly and courteously when I email them."

"On all levels, agents in the creative industry reply promptly and courteously when I email them."

"Deserve" Affirmations

"On all levels, I deserve a positive and creatively constructive response when I email a producer."

"On all levels, I deserve a response when I email a producer."

"On all levels, I deserve abundant success as a writer."

"On all levels, I deserve acknowledgement as a writer."

"On all levels, my writing deserves acknowledgement."

"On all levels, creativity is a gift and blessing from the Creator and I deserve to be well-paid for my work."

"On all levels, I deserve to be taken seriously as a writer by producers, screenwriting managers and agents in the creative industry."

"On all levels, my creative work deserves to be lauded and celebrated."

"On all levels, I deserve to be lauded and celebrated as a writer."

"On all levels, I deserve abundant opportunities to have my creative projects and franchises produced."

"On all levels, I deserve to communicate with producers, screenwriting managers and agents in the creative industry who are highly enthusiastic about my creative projects and franchises."

"On all levels, producers, screenwriting managers and agents in the creative industry deserve to be highly enthusiastic about my creative projects and franchises."

"On all levels, I deserve to be amazed and astounded by the abundance of opportunities available to me to have my creative projects and franchises produced."

"On all levels, producers, screenwriting managers and agents in the creative industry deserve to be amazed and astounded by my creative talent and the quality of my creative projects and franchises."

"On all levels, I deserve to be discovered as a writer by producers, directors and creative company CEOs and the Creator intends this for me."

"On all levels, I deserve all creative opportunities that I desire and I can choose how successful I want to be."

Affirmations Starting With 'I love…'

"On all levels, I love receiving praise about my creative writing."

"On all levels, I love being praised for my creativity."

"On all levels, I love making creative breakthroughs."

"On all levels, I love being creative."

"On all levels, I love exploring my creative potential."

"On all levels, I love having creative freedom."

"On all levels, I love achieving creative writing targets that I set for myself."

"On all levels, I love having a wonderfully fertile imagination for creative writing."

"On all levels, I love growing and evolving as a writer."

"On all levels, I love feeling satisfaction with my creative achievements."

"On all levels, I love being successful with my creative writing."

"On all levels, I love being a successful writer."

"On all levels, I love receiving positive feedback about one of my scripts/creative works."

Miscellaneous Affirmations

"On all levels, the creative industry is unable to ignore the irresistible appeal of my unique and distinct voice as a writer."

"On all levels, my unique and distinct

voice as a writer is highly sought after by producers, screenwriting managers and agents in the creative industry."

"On all levels, the creative industry deserves to benefit from my unique and distinct voice as a writer."

"On all levels, my unique and distinct voice as a writer is widely lauded and celebrated within the creative industry."

"On all levels, producers, screenwriting managers and agents in the creative industry are unable to ignore the irresistible appeal of my unique and distinct voice as a writer."

"On all levels, my wisdom and insight as a writer are greatly admired."

"On all levels, the creative industry deserves to benefit from my admirable wisdom and insight as a writer."

"On all levels, I am successful."

"On all levels, I am a successful writer."

"On all levels, I am achieving ever greater success as a writer."

Mini-Dictionary

In this chapter I've included some definitions for some words and terms which may be helpful.

Allusion
An allusion is where an event, character, item, location, title, etc from the same or another creative work are hinted at but not referenced specifically. 'Biblical allusions', for example, would be stories or dialogue that are reminiscent of the Bible but don't reference any specific part of the Bible. A reference is where an event, character, item, location, title etc from the same or another creative work are mentioned specifically. 'Biblical references' would mean a creative work quotes specific Bible passages, while 'Biblical allusions' would be vague hints that suggest specific Bible passages without referencing them specifically.

In regards to mentioning names of characters from another

creative work, or mentioning the title of another creative work, as I understand it, like with song titles where you're allowed to mention song titles and the name of the singer without needing permission, you can mention characters from another creative work as long as 1. it's not defamatory of the work that character originates from 2. Neither that character nor a character with the same name appears in any of your creative works without permission from the relevant copyright holder (e.g. you can have a character mention that they like Batman, especially if you're mentioning a specific Batman movie, comic book, video game, etc, but you cannot have the character Batman appear in your work or have a character with the same name without permission).

Bit Part
A character role that has either no or hardly any dialogue who's unimportant to the plot. Too many of these characters in a single script would be a sign of bad writing and such a script could benefit from being revised to remove such characters. More bit parts = more wasted screen time.

-esque
When you encounter a word ending in -esque, my understanding of what that word means is:
"Designed to imitate, usually in a flattering way and is 'reminiscent' of what it imitates"
Romanesque – named after the Roman Empire, and the Roman Empire itself was named after the city of Rome (and even further back there's a story about the origin of the name

of that city, but I will leave the reader to research that at their leisure). An example would be 'Romanesque architecture'.

Tolkienesque – named after J.R.R Tolkien, imitates Middle Earth, Lord of the Rings, and/or Tolkien's constructed languages.

Exposition
Content that explains in detail important information about a character, event, item, etc – (an) extended flashback(s) revealing character backstory, a character explaining a topic in great detail, items in video games such as books, letters, emails, audio tapes, etc, are examples of exposition. An 'info dump' is where there is what might be perceived as excessive exposition – frequent 'info dumps' aren't necessarily inexcusable in and of themselves, but if the 'info dumps' are particularly long – for example, in a TV show - a full episode or multiple episodes, in a book - a full chapter or longer, in a video game - an especially long cutscene or series of cutscenes (remember that Metal Gear Solid 4 series of cutscenes mentioned before? Avoid *that* sort of exposition by any means necessary!), then it can become a sign that characters' backstories or the plot are becoming too complex. Try to keep 'info dumps' sparse and when they *are* present, remember Shakespeare's quote about brevity!

Filler
Content which doesn't further the main plot in any way. In anime based on a manga, filler is any material which doesn't appear in the manga, which is used to allow the in-progress

manga's story to get ahead of the anime. Filler sometimes gives extra screen time to characters who otherwise don't appear very often.

Flashforward
Essentially the opposite of a flashback, where instead of past events are revealed, future events are revealed. Often when this is used, particularly if it's a movie or video game, some, most or even all of the story is catching up to the events shown in the flashforward, depending on how far in advance the events of the flashforward were. This can sometimes be used for foreshadowing.

Foreshadowing
Foreshadowing is when a major event, plot twist, or character/villain reveal is hinted at in advance. A complete lack of foreshadowing might mean a major villain suddenly appears unexpectedly, while excessive foreshadowing (frequent hints at the plot twist, or character/villain reveal) could undermine the impact of the event. Foreshadowing works best when it's reasonably subtle, for example when there are subtle hints about a villain before his/her appearance. An example of poor foreshadowing is a movie or video game villain who only appears at the end and where little or none of their backstory or personality is revealed before the movie or video game's ending.

-ian/-an
I'm not sure how applicable it is to non-English languages,

but in the English language at least, creative writing can (and attempt to where possible) create words ending in - '-ian' and '-an' can be added to many words or a name to make it a demonym (name of a person from a particular place) e.g. Philadelphian 'person from the U.S city of Philadelphia' or a group, occupation e.g. Russian: 'from Russia', Historian 'person who studies history', Politician 'person involved in politics', Dickensian 'of or reminiscent of the works of Charles Dickens', Freudian 'relating to or influenced by Sigmund Freud' (origin of the expression 'Freudian slip'). However, there are exceptions, and some are quite rare. for example: Portugal 'Portuguese', Japan 'Japanese', China 'Chinese' not 'Chinian' or 'Chinan', New Yorker 'from New York', Glaswegian 'Glasgow', Londonite 'London'.

-ist/-ism or -er
Again, I'm not sure how applicable it is to non-English languages, but in English almost any word can have -ist or -ism added to it. Adding -er to a word that doesn't have an -er ending in English could also work in some situations.

Neologisms
The layman definition would be 'newly-coined words, phrases or expressions' or newly *invented* if you prefer – as in, if a new word is invented, once the first notable person to use it in some situation or after the first notable use of it in Popular Culture, it becomes a neologism – 'notable' meaning that two high school students inventing a new word in a phone call

between them, or two 'gamers' (people who are avid video game players – I don't know how well the word 'gamer' translates into non-English languages, and I also don't know the Japanese word used to refer to them) using a neologism in voice chat during an online gaming session - these are not considered notable people for the purposes of establishing earliest usages of such neologisms, and any neologisms they made in that context are not officially recognised.

Pseudo-
Intended to imitate, for example, pseudo-3D, or not (or at least not currently) existing in real-life (does not exist in a non-fictional context) – I intentionally chose not to say 'the real world', because I've noticed that the phrase 'the real world' has been used – especially by authority figures - with many condescending connotations e.g. 'let me teach you how things work in the real world', 'it could never work in the real world', 'he/she isn't living in the real world'.

Unfortunately, this has a particularly negative connotation when considering science and spirituality, as 'pseudo-science' is often applied by the scientific community to anything with even a whiff of being considered a 'spiritual' notion. If something with a mere *whiff* of spirituality is 'pseudo-science', those scientists' *attitude* has a *stench* of atheism. My view is that throwing the phrase 'pseudo-science' around without restraint can actually be harmful.

I prefer the definition of 'intending to imitate but of inferior quality to the real thing' used by technology – a product claimed to utilise 'pseudo 3D' means it imitates 3D but isn't true 3D.

Pseudonym (also known as 'pen name', or 'alias') doesn't have a particularly negative connotation despite pseudo being Greek for 'false' – in fact, pseudonym translates to 'false name' – you generally don't hear authors being called 'frauds' for using a pseudonym or 'false name' like how spirituality attracts the 'pseudo-science' label!

Option Agreement
An Option Agreement is where a producer has read a script and wants to produce that project, but doesn't currently have the funds to produce it. Option Agreements will contain contract clauses, and it may be beneficial for a writer to request that they maintain exclusive rights to script revisions, and the right to approve or veto sequels, prequels, remakes, spin-offs, TV show adaptations, etc as well as exclusive rights to be the writer of any sequels, prequels, remakes, spin-offs or TV adaptations. For a movie Option Agreement, consider suggesting to the producer that you'll agree to a 'conditional $0 agreement', with the condition being that you'll receive no money from the purchase but must receive a 'backend' (percentage of box office gross) – try to negotiate for 10% of box office gross. If your creative work is already intended as a franchise (particularly TV series or video game franchise), consider putting a non-negotiable clause in your contract that forbids any 'reboots' of that franchise.

Similes
Similes are often misunderstood as meaning the same thing

as a metaphor, but the English word 'simile' is derived from the Latin word 'similis' (think 'similar'), and for something to count as a simile it must contain 'X is like' or 'Like X, Y…', e.g. 'Her hair is like silk', 'His room looks like a warzone'. Some similes contain "as [insert adjective] as a/an [insert noun], e.g. 'As tough as an ox'.

Subplot
A part of a story that's secondary to the main plot and can either develop separately from the main story or can feed into it. Subplots can sometimes involve supporting characters instead of main characters. A romantic subplot is a common type of subplot. Subplots can also be interconnected where events in one subplot affect another, and vice versa.

Subtext
Subtext is any meaning in a creative work which is implicit (in other words, not specifically stated or depicted – which would be explicit meaning). Subtext can inform the audience about a character, the plot and even the context of the plot. One use of subtext is to convey emotion that isn't communicated directly through a character's words or actions.

Tweaking
Tweaking is when you revise a completed first draft of a script or novel to improve dialogue, improve humour or make adjustments to a creative project's plot. A single script or novel might be tweaked on multiple different occasions – generally, there will be more tweaks if the first draft is of lower quality

and there will be fewer tweaks if the first draft was of higher quality. A writer's early creative projects may tend to require more tweaks than their more recent creative projects.

Unreliable Narrator
A type of narration where the version of events narrated is not necessarily the true version of events – for example some details being open to interpretation, some details being omitted, or some details being embellished. This is best used when the narrating character is of questionable character such as a villain or former villain, or is trying to hide something that the true version of events would reveal – do *not* use this trope for a character you want the audience to perceive as trustworthy.

Writing Tips

I learned many lessons about writing the 'near-Mission Impossible way' through trial and error with no help or advice at all from anyone else, and the intention with this book was to give other writers a 'Quick-Start Guide' for writers who are 'starting out', so they can learn from the trial and error I went through, particularly earlier on. They were originally posted on my creative writing blog, zheretblog.wordpress.com but some have been tweaked, and I've added many extra tips that weren't on my blog. Here are my 'pro tips':

- **Decide** on Genre before you do anything else - *or* start writing first, see what develops from 'early work', *then* decide on Genre. A memorable and/or unique title, though not mandatory, helps in part to form the work's identity - preferably a title of 1,2 or 3 words [excluding a subtitle]. Avoid writing crime shows or murder mysteries as there's already an overabundance of them, there's not a lot new that can be done with them that hasn't already been done (murder mysteries in particular have been done to death [pun intended]), and murder mysteries in particular could stifle your imagination and creativity and not offer much of a chance for you to flex your creative muscle.

- **Research** other things in the same genre and avoid clichés and overused/recycled tropes where possible (visit the TV Tropes website for examples). Aim for originality in a particular genre where you can (e.g. don't make a 'zombie' story full of clichés that adds nothing new to the zombie genre just because zombies might be popular). Also, read plenty of books to get a handle on writing.

- **Consider** the relationship/balance between factors such as originality, execution, and delivery (examples: a brilliantly original plot can be let down by melodramatic delivery and/or poor dialogue, a moderately original/slightly unoriginal plot with excellent execution and a unique delivery can become something 'fresh') – think 'gestalt' (the whole being greater than the sum of its individual parts).

- (Optional) **Spiritualise**: When aiming to incorporate spiritual elements/spirituality of any kind, they should ideally be as **accessible, relevant,** and **relatable** as possible (and if possible/where applicable, **contemporary** as well), and not be 'fluff'. While they **can** be 'made up' (i.e. not based on existing information, beliefs or concepts in spirituality circles), they **must** make sense and **must** be consistent in their internal logic - and ideally something the audience can easily grasp (i.e. not 'New Age-y' or esoteric in any obvious way), or you'll alienate a wider and more mainstream audience and your work will only reach a niche audience. You must find a style, presentation and genre that are suitable for expressing those spiritual elements - if it doesn't come across as overtly spiritual, you've done your job (comedy might be helpful for this).

(Stargate SG-1 is a good example of well-incorporated spiritual elements.)

- **Make** an effort to write **every** day (or close as possible to every day); 1-2 hours minimum, and ideally longer (3 hours if possible). Having a rough idea or plan what you're going to write or work on *before* you start writing rather than trying to figure everything out on the spot while you're writing means your writing will be easier, quicker, more efficient and better quality. Try to have plot outlines before you start writing scripts, even if the outlines are only dot point lists.

- **Always** keep a notebook handy to record ideas, or type up notes on computer if you don't like handwriting, and keep regular, up-to-date backups of your work via USB stick as well as an external hard drive.

- **Avoid** unnecessary 'throw-away' scenes that have no dialogue (or at least no significant dialogue) and where virtually nothing happens (e.g. 1. a character on the street walking to the entrance of a building before meeting (a) person/people inside, 2. a character is sitting in a waiting room 3. a character walks up to their car and enters before starting to drive) *unless* they have importance to the overall plot, or are part of a subplot (e.g. 1. the character is attacked, meets someone or receives an important phone call or text 2. something significant or unexpected happens in the waiting room 3. something important happens in the car park, or an important sign or visual clue in the car park of later importance needs to be revealed), and learn to 'cut' to locations/interiors of locations seamlessly.

- **Avoid** 'bit part' characters, especially if they only have 2-3 lines of dialogue in an entire script unless for whatever reason that character is essential to the plot. Try to avoid including any unnecessary characters, especially if you're writing an ultra-low budget movie – there's no point wasting screen time on any characters that aren't necessary for development of the plot. Some exceptions would be if a character is crucial to a particular subplot, and obviously in military battles there are almost no limits to the number of on-screen characters, but for military battles, focus only on important characters.

- A Golden Rule of sorts that I made up: "Don't put all your eggs into one basket creatively, but don't create original I.Ps without restraint either". Anything shoehorned into an existing series that doesn't really fit can work better as an original I.P where those ideas, themes, subject matter, etc are present from the beginning and can be fleshed out and expanded and are not squandered be being shoehorned into an existing I.P, while you preferably only create original I.Ps if the material, subject matter, genre, etc are completely incompatible with an existing I.P.

- While dialogue is generally the least essential aspect of writing (except for comedies where it's the most important aspect), having intelligent and clever dialogue improves the overall quality - even a brilliant, innovative plot can be tarnished by awful dialogue. Bad dialogue is *much* easier to tweak/fix than a bad plot. Practice writing song lyrics (or poetry, if that works better for you) to improve your ability to write succinct, high-quality dialogue which requires fewer words/sentences yet conveys more meaning - see how much meaning you can fit using as few words as possible.

- If a script can still be tweaked, it's not ready. Do **not** submit first drafts to producers, screenwriting managers or agents. Returning to 'old' scripts when you're more experienced should allow you to review it objectively – you might be surprised how much further some of your scripts can be tweaked!

- Quoting a well-known expression doesn't usually count as originality, as some of these expressions have been quoted so often in TV shows, movies, books, even video games in some cases, that they are considered cliché (e.g. 'hell hath no fury like a woman scorned'). If you can bring originality to a well-known expression by adding a twist to it, or a pun, etc, this is better than simply including well-known expressions word-for-word to give a false impression of a character's or writer's wisdom.

- If something can be reworked or tweaked, particularly to allow the introduction of new characters, plot elements, subplots, locations, humour/jokes, backstory, etc, then do so and work the new material/ideas **around** your existing work - try to avoid scrapping work you've already done and starting over from scratch or worse yet, scrapping whole projects entirely. You can revise, edit, tweak etc as much as you want but once (or if) something's been produced it usually can't be changed (esp. movies, books, and TV shows). Sometimes something as simple as changing or tweaking a project's title can give you more freedom with that project.

- If you feel you have no choice but to scrap a project entirely, 'don't throw the baby out with the bath water' – in other words, if there is anything *at all* worth salvaging from that project before you scrap it, such as any sections of dialogue you're fond of, character names you'd like to keep, original location names, etc, then create a Microsoft Word document or a new script file and copy and paste the salvaged content into that file. You might end up creating a project where the salvaged content works better than it did in the scrapped project.

- When tweaking dialogue, try to focus on one or more of the following:

1. Adding extra information about a character, the main plot or a subplot, a location, the history of the overall setting, an important object (a relic or artifact, a legendary weapon, etc), terminology (especially in a Sci-Fi or Fantasy setting), etc
2. Adding in humour (or, if it's a comedic project, *improving* humour anywhere the script has flat dialogue except any dialogue that's important to the plot), even if it's only dry humour, also known as 'deadpan humour'
3. Expressing a character's personality, especially if their earliest appearance was brief and gave little idea of that character's personality

- When possible, let tweaked dialogue be 'informed' or 'guided' by existing dialogue, and rework inarticulate or 'clunky' dialogue to make it more eloquent rather than always replacing dialogue with entirely new dialogue when tweaking. Beware 'clunkers' (clunky phrases and sentences)!

- Depending on genre or plot, if a particular country or culture is involved, buy a language dictionary (Can't emphasise this enough! Especially if you can find one for cheap!) and see what you can use - this can either be dialogue where they speak that language (e.g. a historical drama set in Russia), or sometimes a specific word, phrase or expression in a particular language will 'jump out at you' and you feel you need to find some way to use it.

- If creating (an) original culture(s) and/or constructed language(s), consider purchasing The Language Construction Kit, and The Planet Construction Kit, and later the Advanced Language Construction Kit and The Conlanger's Lexipedia, as well as the Game of Thrones conlanger's book The Art of Language Invention (possibly even start with that book first). Mark Rosenfelder's books are generally fairly useful, but you'll probably get *limited* benefit from the Syntax Construction Kit (or at least *I* did).

- When creating original character names, search for their full names on the internet and make sure they are *not* names of celebrities, not even athletes, because a. the names would not be original (you want *original* character names, right?) b. you can avoid those characters being confused for those celebrities c. you won't get sued if you avoid using them.

- **Find** your 'style' - there are creative people who have a signature style that makes them unique, and are influenced by different things. Find out what these are and 'work to your strengths'. If particular things were an influence, try to incorporate those influences in a way that fits with your creative style, but differentiate your project(s) as much as possible from what they were influenced by and give your project(s) as much distinctiveness as possible rather than create an obvious knock-off of something else - avoid being generic or uninspired: aim to be original, distinct, and unique. Feel free to experiment with things such as: acronyms whose initials form a complete word; interesting/memorable anagrams (including a word or name spelt backwards); ironic character names, clever (and importantly, original) portmanteaus; self-aware humour.

- **Use** good judgement in regards to using slang and vocabulary of foreign language speakers in dialogue, avoid characters who speak almost entirely in slang as it can make such characters appear stupid and immature. Slang can be useful (or even at its *most* useful) when writing comedy, especially if you're English-speaking. For foreign language speakers, don't just pepper their dialogue with foreign words – include maybe one or two words from their native language per sentence unless they're speaking to other foreigners who speak the same language.

- **Be** patient with 'getting your work out there' and hearing people telling you (repeatedly) to 'get a 'real' job as opposed to a 'fake job' (because obviously being 'creative' counts as a 'fake job' in some people's books) and don't give up if you get rejected again and again - someone *eventually* will be able to tell if you have potential! It's meaningful even if some people are 'time burglars'. If you have a passion for writing or find it fulfilling, remember the famous Nike slogan!

- **Take** regular breaks - have something to eat/drink, meditate, listen to music, whatever you need to do to keep focused.

- **Don't** feel you have to rush to 'get things done on time' whatever your definition of 'on time' is - take as long as you need to avoid a 'rush job': "A delayed game is eventually good, but a rushed game is forever bad." - Shigeru Miyamoto, Creative Fellow at Nintendo (Though the quote is about video games, the same logic can be applied to many other creative mediums).

- **Invest** in a comprehensive (and up-to-date!) English dictionary, even if you're a native English speaker, and keep it on hand in case you come across a word online or in a book that you aren't familiar with, especially if it's a long or obscure English word. The Oxford English Dictionary is accepted as the most reputable, and its contributors decide which new words are officially accepted and added to the English language and which words are rejected from being officially added to the English language. Also, try exploring http://phrontistery.info/index.html to research archaic and obsolete English words.

- If you're 'into comedy', watch comedies you enjoy and get an idea of what YOU, not 'other people' define as 'good comedy'. Also, don't rely on puns on their own for humour - most of the humour from puns comes from how they're used, not so much the puns themselves.

- If you've completed a first draft of a movie or video game script, consider printing it off and going through it thoroughly a page at a time. Try ticking sections of dialogue that don't need tweaking and for any dialogue that needs tweaking, circle it, or put an X or asterisk near it, whatever works for you.

- **Before** sending a producer, screenwriting manager or agent a query email about a movie script, TV series, or video game script, make sure the first page of the script is as well-written as it can be because I've read online that producers, screenwriting managers, and agents will often stop reading a script after the first page if the first page of the script is dull or has poor quality writing (or even worse, typos!). If you try submitting such a script, the script might go mostly unread and you'd be unlikely to receive further communication from that gatekeeper.

- When writing dialogue, possibly the biggest mistake to avoid is characters that either sound the same or sound too similar and who lack their own 'voice'. If you can mentally read dialogue between two or more characters and if you pretend the character names are hidden, find it difficult to tell characters apart from each other (and anyone in the creative industry who reads your scripts is likely to pick up on that problem), then revise until the characters' personalities and vocabulary are distinct from each other.

- Try to 'be bold' whenever possible in relation to themes, plot, dialogue and characters – be unafraid for your projects to 'make a statement' (in a positive way), but don't forget to be mindful of taboos.

- Script assessment services (where you pay to have a script assessed and receive notes on what can be improved, what things 'aren't working' with your script, etc) might be helpful but there are costs involved and there is a certain amount of turnaround time on your script assessment (generally several weeks). Don't use those services if you have a large number of TV show scripts (cost and turnaround time would be prohibitive), but **consider** using them if you have a movie or video game script that you're particularly 'stuck' with and don't know how to go about improving it – the script assessor's notes might include things you hadn't considered! Make sure the script assessment service you're planning to use is reputable first, though.

- I apologise in advance if this sounds 'cold', but I'd advise caution about requesting friends or family members to read your creative writing, for the following reasons:
1. If they don't like your writing, they might be too afraid of hurting your feelings to be able to criticise your work
2. They might be quite 'blunt' if they think your writing is terrible rather than offering constructive criticism
3. If they like your writing, they probably won't be qualified to give you detailed feedback or critique your work (unless that person is a writer themself)
4. Family members or friends are unlikely to be helpful at giving you suggestions on how to improve your writing

- Use repetition of words and/or sections of dialogue and/or complete sentences sparingly, particularly if the word is written more than twice consecutively – exceptions would be phrases like 'going, going, gone' and 'location, location, location', or in song lyrics, where a certain amount of repetition can be acceptable e.g. the song 'Row, Row, Row Your

Boat'. An exception to repetition is a character repeating or paraphrasing a quote by another character earlier in that creative work, which is usually used for dramatic effect, but don't overdo it.

- When tweaking a completed first draft, try allocating a certain amount of time that you feel is reasonable for completing the tweaking. I had a movie script I was particularly stuck on for years (the one I mentioned I tweaked the names with), which I allocated a '6 Week Polish Plan' to tweak (that's polish as in nail polish, not Poland). I had many breakthroughs with that script, and only needed about two and a half of the 6 weeks I'd allocated. I also allocated a '3 Week Polish Plan' for an 8-episode storyline that I reworked into a movie.

- Don't have characters mentioning other characters' names in dialogue frequently, especially if it's not for a specific reason. A character's name should generally only be mentioned in dialogue in the following circumstances: two or more characters are meeting for the first time and are being introduced to each other (or regular characters are meeting an unfamiliar character for the first time and need to be introduced to each other); dramatic effect (e.g. a character is angry with another character, or sad, excited, grateful, a character needs to ask another character a question and there are more than two characters present, etc), or comedic effect.

- Some alternatives to writing crime genre or murder mysteries are musicals, Hack and Slash video games and alternative history (fictional versions of history that had different outcomes. If you have a good concept for an alternative history, use it!).

- If you're a Japanese writer and planning to have characters with Western names, consider researching to see if the name is common in the West – Final Fantasy VI had to change a character's name in the West because her name in the Japanese version was a common name in the West but was considered exotic in Japan. If it's a relatively uncommon or even rare name even in the West, you're all set!

- Sibling Names: Siblings often have names that rhyme, start with the same letter or end with the same letter.

- If you're planning to write video game scripts, consider the book Game Writing: Narrative Skills For Video Games a must-read.

- Silent Protagonist (mostly in video games): If you want to write a video game that has a Silent Protagonist, try to have as many dialogue options and Choice and Consequence decisions as possible to give the impression of the Silent Protagonist interacting with the in-game world (Elder Scrolls does it quite well, while in the Legend of Zelda games, due to lack of Choice and Consequence and lack of dialogue options, Link can seem a bit like an automaton at times [dialogue options in Legend of Zelda games are typically 'Yes' or 'No' responses to questions from an NPC]).

- When to cut content from a script: Generally, cutting content from a script will be from movie scripts, as due to technology nowadays with video games, there are very few occasions where a video game script or video game itself will require content to be CUT in order to fit on the media format (cutting content from video games was common until around the PS2 era by my observations). You should be fairly conservative with cutting content from movie scripts rather than making 'savage' cuts, and what you should be aiming to 'cut' are any scenes that are 'dead weight' that are either: a: not furthering the main plot, or, b: not related to a subplot.

- A writer MIGHT be able to get the attention of the creative industry by producing a short film, but the script for that short film would have to be anywhere from 'solid' to 'excellent' - a poorly made, poorly written short film would probably just get ignored by the creative industry.

- First Person Perspective vs. Third Person Perspective: It's unlikely you'll ever find yourself in a situation where you'll write a creative work in first person. First Person Perspective in creative writing is quite restrictive, as the narrative is only able to show either events the character narrating experienced first-hand, or conversations the character narrating may have overheard, or possibly things the character *read* about. Some creative works may lend themselves to being written in First Person Perspective, but fairly rarely.

- Linearity vs Non-Linearity (in video games): A consideration that needs to be made if considering non-linearity is narrative – generally, the more non-linear a video game is, the less complex the story (as a story, by nature, is linear). A highly non-linear video game (for example, Legend of Zelda: Breath of the Wild) requires a relatively minimalist story – a highly developed (and linear) narrative would restrict a game's ability to be non-linear).

- If paranormal elements are involved with a particular project, aim for believability rather than realism – unprecedented *imagination* will do a **lot** more for your creativity than unprecedented *realism*. For example, if one or more of your creative works feature magic, give serious consideration to details like what in-universe rules and limitations (and possibly even in-universe taboos) there are regarding magic – don't give magic unlimited capability without any restrictions, this will jeopardise believability. Another example: if one or more of your creative works feature ghosts, give ghosts believable capabilities (ghosts might have some abilities living characters don't have, but might also have certain limitations) with believable knowledge – don't make a ghost seemingly all-knowing. A ghost is still a person, not a god.

- Clarification about character limits for character names: aim to keep characters' first names shorter than 11 characters (a 10-character limit), particularly if you're planning to write an RPG. In rare circumstances, you might be able to allow a 12-character limit. Surnames are allowed to be longer than 10 characters as they're less commonly used than first names (surnames will probably appear rarely in a video game – in an RPG, it's unlikely surnames will appear in battles), but keep surnames under 15 characters long if possible. If a character has an absurdly long name, humour might be appropriate.

- If you're writing a TV series, especially if it's intended as a long-running series, for movies, as often as possible, aim for an original story rather than retelling a pre-existing storyline from the series, an extended movie-length version of a specific episode (if the series is an hour-long show) or worse yet, taking content from existing episodes and editing them into a movie with (usually) only a small amount of original content (if it has any original content at all). Unless a pre-existing storyline is being told from a different perspective (such as a supporting character or a villain), and there is enough original content to justify a such movie, then you can experiment a little, but original content is usually preferable to recycled content.

- Be careful not to get confused by words that are spelt the same, but pronounced differently or words that are spelt the same and pronounced the same but have a different meaning, especially in English (some English words have multiple different meanings). This is something that could lend itself to humour, particularly if you find words in English that have a word in another language with the same spelling and/or pronounciation that has a completely different meaning.

- Be open to using rhyming and alliteration (a sequence of words in a sentence or a phrase that start with the same letter), especially if you're English-speaking. You might sometimes find a use for rhymes in dialogue or even episode titles (if you're working on a TV series) or chapter titles (if you're working on a novel), and alliteration can be useful in some situations.

- Avoid excessive swearing, use swearing sparingly and generally only have characters swear either for emphasis or when frustrated.

- In real life, scientific classifications of plants and animals are generally in Latin, and many medical and technology-related words are derived from Greek. If you have any cultures in any of your works based on the Romans or Greeks, those languages are fair game, but if you have a creative work featuring alien races, if they have exotic plant and animal life, you could create a constructed language used by that alien race for scientific classification and the same, or another, constructed language can be used for that alien race's medical and technology-related words. Also, with any word containing –mancy, the preceding word is almost always derived from Greek, so too with –phobia.

- Ballet and fencing terminology generally come from French, as do many culinary terms. Furthermore, many musical terms come from Italian, many legal terms come from Latin, etc.

- If you're English-speaking, be mindful of linguistic differences between U.S, U.K and Australian English. Non-U.S varieties of English tend to conform to UK English spelling conventions, but in addition, Australian English has a rather distinct variety of slang, as well as some words borrowed from Australian Aboriginal languages such as boomerang, didgeridoo, and kangaroo.

- Make every effort to use the proper name for a particular group of animals e.g. a pride of lions, a parliament of owls.

- Silent films: It's unlikely you'll ever write a movie that's completely silent with no dialogue whatsoever, but if for whatever reason you do write one, your movie will need a compelling plot and hopefully can be made as visually diverse as possible to avoid long stretches of the same scenery. Without dialogue, long stretches with the same or similar scenery is something some people might find boring (not everyone who watches movies likes silent films).

- On a similar note, occasional scenes with no dialogue are much more acceptable. Not every scene automatically requires dialogue – sometimes a scene containing only a visual cue is sufficient, but try to avoid making the visual cue too subtle (there definitely *is* such a thing as being *too* subtle).

- On yet another similar note, occasionally, a gesture or body language might be more effective to convey a response or emotion than half a page or more of dialogue. Gestures include: thumbs up/thumbs down, the slit throat gesture, the rude finger, a wink, a nod, spitting, etc.

- Regarding themes in your creative works, try to avoid the extremes of either the themes being too subtle or the other extreme of the themes being hammered in frequently (often through dialogue rather than plot or action). Try thinking of themes as a kind of subtext – try to *imply* rather than being explicit. Themes might develop before the plot (if you had specific themes in mind before you started a particular project), but the reverse can sometimes be true (especially, if you just starting started writing a project to see what developed from your early work). If the reverse is true of one of your projects, see if you can pick up on any clues in your work that suggest which themes might be dominant (for example, if particular topics occur frequently in dialogue but at that point in the plot are not being explored by the plot, that might be one way of figuring out the future direction of the plot), and explore those themes further as the project develops. Alternatively, themes could be explored by subplots, or, in the case of video games, in optional content.

- If you're planning to have one or more creative works based on mythology, when you feel confident enough, you can try constructed mythology where you invent new additions to an existing mythology, just make sure your additions are compatible with the mythology. You could even choose to declare your additions to the mythology Public Domain if you're prepared to let other people use that constructed mythology you invented. For convenience, try to stick with a mythology with a language still spoken in the Twenty-First Century – a mythology with an extinct language (e.g. Egyptian, Sumerian) might be difficult to create new myths for due to lack of access to an up-to-date dictionary for that language.

- Sexual innuendo should generally be subtle and tasteful humour regarding innuendo is preferable to more vulgar sexual references.

- Medical dramas: These will typically be TV shows (or possibly novels, occasionally video games, but rarely movies). If you're planning to write a medical drama, keep in mind that a lot of the writing will be pre-existing medical jargon and the main thing you'll be 'inventing' will be the characters. If this sounds too creatively stifling, then don't write medical dramas.

- Children's TV shows: Some children's TV shows have 5 or 10 minute episodes, so brevity would be a prerequisite. Another thing common with children's TV shows is a 'half hour' episode length which is divided into two different storylines, or 'segments'. You might find children's TV shows less creatively stifling than things such as murder mysteries and medical dramas.

- Animated series: If you're considering an animated series, I'd strongly advise mature content as Western animated TV shows rarely have a mature age rating (with a small number of exceptions), in contrast to anime, and contributing to exploring possibilities with mature content in Western animation is a worthy goal. I would also suggest considering having your animated series produced as a comic book/graphic novel series first to reduce risk, and it would be helpful to make such a decision as early on as possible.

- Based on a true story: If you know a story that would work well as a movie that hasn't already been the basis of a movie, keep in mind it must follow the real-life events as closely as possible, and isn't the place for unrestricted imagination.

- Publishing options: Nowadays, traditional publishing is not the only option for publishing. There are three types of publishing: traditional, self-publishing, and hybrid publishing (which combines elements of both traditional publishing and self-publishing). With traditional publishing, the publisher covers the publishing costs but might be very particular about who or what they will or won't publish, the author receives an 'advance' and receives no royalties until their book has earned in sales at least the amount of the advance, the author generally has little to no input regarding cover design, the publisher takes a certain amount of creative control of the author's book, etc. A traditional publisher might insist on an author having a contract to keep writing novels, including deadlines for completion – if that sounds like an unacceptable amount of pressure for you, consider either self-publishing or hybrid publishing.

With self-publishing, you must complete the entire publishing process yourself, including finding someone to work on the cover design. You must also finance every aspect of the publishing process out of your own money. You also receive the least amount of help from a publisher (since you don't *have* one if you choose this option).

With hybrid-publishing, you pay the publisher to publish your book (relatively inexpensive compared to ultra-low budget movies), and they guide you through the publishing process, including helping with the cover design. You're able to still make corrections to your manuscript during the publishing process, but depending on how many corrections are needed, it may cost extra. Book promotion services are a *must* if going with this option if you want sales as your book will be essentially online only.

Traditional publishers have the best distribution model out of the three – your book *will* appear in bricks-and-mortar bookstores with a traditional publisher, but are probably the hardest to succeed at publishing with. Self-publishing requires the most amount of effort and the author needs to know more-or-less exactly what they're doing regarding the publishing process.

Depending on your financial situation, hybrid publishing might be worth considering, because you can publish almost anything within reason (except song lyrics used without permission, as mentioned earlier, and, I assume, no slander or libel), and convincing a traditional publisher to consider your book has the potential to be quite difficult. With self-publishing and hybrid publishing, you maintain almost complete creative control over your book – think of it as a way of potentially getting at least some of your creative work out there in the world!

- Some websites about creative writing recommend reading

scripts that are available on the internet to learn how to write rather than simply watching a lot of movies. The scripts of a selection of highly-regarded movies have been made available to read for free online, but make sure the website is reputable before you try to read any scripts. Reading scripts, especially of any of highly-regarded movies, will teach you a *lot* more about screenwriting than watching a lot of movies and TV shows and playing a lot of video games. Importantly, you'll learn what a correctly formatted script looks like.

- Memorise that Shakespeare quote about brevity, or alternatively, simply write a reminder to use brevity whenever and wherever possible (but don't overdo it – brevity should be used where it's *appropriate* but not when it would be *in*appropriate). Yes, brevity is *that* important!

- Try keeping an A4 exercise book near your bed in case you need to urgently write notes about a project to avoid forgetting the details later. Luckily, A4 exercise books are very affordable and have a variety of page counts, so it might be advisable to stock up on them.

- Guest characters (a feature in some RPGs, occasionally in some other genres) are characters who accompany the party and participate in battle, but who permanently leave the party at some point and cannot be re-recruited (a permanent character, on the other hand, might leave the party on one or more occasions but re-joins the party at some point). For example, a guest character might join for a specific dungeon then leave when that dungeon is completed, or might remain for a significant portion of the game. Three things you'll need to decide regarding Guest characters are: how many

Guest characters your RPG will have; when each Guest character joins the party; when each Guest character leaves the party. In your RPG script, when a Guest character first joins, type (without the quotation marks) something along the lines of "GUEST CHARACTER, [INSERT NAME OF CHARACTER], JOINS THE PARTY", and when a Guest character leaves the party, type (without the quotation marks) "GUEST CHARACTER, [INSERT NAME OF CHARACTER], LEAVES THE PARTY".

Often, Guest characters will be A.I controlled meaning the player can't control them in battle, but in some situations, such as a game where a permanent character is being accompanied by more than one Guest character, those Guest characters might be controllable in battle, at least in a turn-based RPG. In some RPGs, Guest character equipment can be removed or altered, in other RPGs, Guest character equipment is inaccessible.

- Be polite and respectful **at all times** during your communication with agents, screenwriting managers and producers, as creative industry gatekeepers do a lot of networking amongst themselves and news of disrespect and bad behaviour by writers might travel very fast within the creative industry and make it (even) harder for such writers to succeed.

- If you have original character names, location names, etc (not derived from an existing language, regardless of whether the name comes from a constructed language or not) or otherwise a name from a real language whose pronounciation is less than obvious (particularly if the spelling is noticeably different than the pronounciation, which is extremely common in Irish, and French has an abundance of silent letters), when you're writing scripts, include the correct pronounciation in brackets directly after the first appearance of that name and also any time an unfamiliar character first speaks it to avoid actors mispronouncing those names. Hypothetically, if you had something produced and actors mispronounced names and you become particularly bothered by it, it's because you didn't take the effort to take the actor's performance into account. Don't say I didn't warn you!

- Regarding nicknames, in more casual situations, it's acceptable to have a character referred to by a nickname frequently or even almost exclusively, but in formal situations (especially any situation where their full name is likely to be mentioned) you would write the character's real first name, then their nickname in quotation marks, then their real surname. Obviously, if for whatever reason a character doesn't *have* a full name, for example, angels, an alien culture who doesn't use surnames, or even Pagan gods, then this rule doesn't apply. A nickname can be obvious, cryptic, quirky, or even humourous – it's up to *you*!

- A couple of extra things you might want to consider if/when writing an RPG script:

1. A gender-balanced main cast (an equal number of playable male and female characters).

2. A female lead character (this is one to use sparingly and not overdo) – a female lead character can be useful in an RPG if expressing emotion openly is important to either the plot or character development for that character, while a male lead character, perhaps even a relatively young one, might be fairly

reserved when it comes to expressing emotion.

- A comedy technique I learned from the High School friend I mentioned in the Contemplating Comedy chapter is saying the opposite of something, including some expressions. However, like the warning about not relying on puns on their own for humour, don't be over-reliant on saying the opposite of something for humour.

- Character name input screens are something you won't be needing when writing for video games unless the video game you're working on will *not* have voice acting (although there are some exceptions – Final Fantasy X allowed inputting a name for the lead character, but the script achieved that by avoiding mentioning his name in dialogue, which some might perceive as unnatural, and some Dragon Quest games such as Dragon Quest VIII and Dragon Quest XI had the ability to input a character name for the lead character, and the voice acting would simply skip that character's name while the subtitles included that character's name). If for whatever reason the video game you're writing has no voice acting, to include character name input screens in your video game script, type something like CHARACTER NAME INPUT SCREEN [DEFAULT: (INSERT CHARACTER NAME)], then PLAYER CONFIRMS CHARACTER NAME: then write whatever follows.

- If you're an atheist writer, please don't take offense at this, but I'd advise keeping your atheism and creative writing separate. Even if you don't believe in anything paranormal whatsoever, still make an effort to be as imaginative as you can. You can have characters who are skeptical, but try to avoid overt atheism in your creative writing. A potential compromise between imagination and realism might be an interpretation of mythology that's very 'grounded'. I firmly believe that with creativity, the idea *should* be to be as imaginative as possible as often as possible, even if you're writing things that seem (highly) implausible or even fantastical. If the audience is entertained, they probably won't be obsessing over realism.

- If you're considering writing comedy, look for patterns such as repetitive or predictable behaviour from a character (or especially *un*predictable behaviour for that matter), foibles and or/ vices that are especially comedic, things that are intended to sound innocent but that have potential to be misinterpreted as sexual innuendo (a character can be oblivious to the innuendo, or can become aware of innuendo at the last minute, or can even be deliberately making double entendres [words or expressions that have a double-meaning, particularly if one is considered innocent and the other innuendo e.g. the nickname 'Dick' for people named Richard, and a certain bird-related word as well as a certain breed of dog]).

- Though I haven't read them myself, there are some Writer's Digest books you might find useful, such as *Crafting Dynamic Dialogue, Creating Characters, Crafting Novels & Short Stories*, and *Writing Voice* – consider those books if you feel like you need more help with your writing than what this book offers. Try investigating the full range of Writer's Digest books and see if there are any that pique your curiosity, you may find things this book doesn't mention.

- If you're an Australian writer, writing movies intended to be produced as Australian movies (as in, movies not released outside Australia or rarely released outside Australia compared to Hollywood movies which, by my observations, have a near-global distribution model) is fine, but if you plan to write either novels or TV shows or both, consider writing content capable of appealing to the general Western audience rather than 'Australiana' content that overseas audiences are unlikely to be interested in. For video games, aim for a global audience rather than the domestic audience unless you're planning to work on games for smartphones and/or tablet devices (the latter two being much more realistic for the Australian video game industry).

- Regarding songs played during a scene, if you know a song that fits the scene, mention it in your script at the start of that scene e.g. [INSERT NAME OF SONG] BY [INSERT NAME OF ARTIST] PLAYS IN BACKGROUND or alternatively [INSERT NAME OF SINGER, BAND OR MUSICIAN]'S [INSERT NAME OF SONG] PLAYS IN BACKGROUND (the 'IN BACKGROUND' part may or may not be necessary), otherwise leave it up to the director or whoever oversees music - consider discussing it with them.

- When a significant section of time is skipped in the script (a 'time skip'), write (without the quotation marks) "ON SCREEN: [Insert number] Day(s)/Week(s)/Month(s)/Year(s) [whichever is relevant] Earlier/Later [whichever is relevant]". Obviously, exclude the parts in brackets. If you're writing a comedy script, you might want to play around with the message that appears on screen to specify the amount of time skipped.

- *Never* accept verbal agreements, especially with contracts

- *always* insist on having it in writing.

- If you're planning to write a comedy TV show, keep the cast size small to medium – since with a fairly large cast, characters compete for screen time and it can be easy for those characters' storylines to barely fit in, let alone any significant humour. The show Parks and Recreation had a fairly large cast, and I noticed that a fair amount of the time, characters were lucky to get a decent amount of screentime and the show was inconsistently humourous. For a comedy TV show, aim for half the cast size of Parks and Recreation, preferably less. Keeping an eye on cast size might be wise even for non-comedic projects, and some genres might accommodate larger casts better than others – not every show can successfully manage a massive ensemble cast like Game of Thrones. Sometimes, there *is* such a thing as too many characters.

- Regarding political satire: with political satire, the humour can become dated quite quickly. Also, depending on your nationality, it might be advisable to avoid satirising real politicians who are still alive, as in some countries (ones that are undemocratic/authoritarian) it might be deemed as dissent which could have serious consequences. In democratic countries, political satire is generally tolerated, but having fictional characters who are only *loosely* based on real politicians (perhaps even characters who are an amalgamation of several different politicians) probably wouldn't be a bad idea.

- Pre-Rendered Cutscenes (mostly video games): Pre-Rendered Cutscenes are cutscenes with greater animation quality than in-game graphics and unlike cutscenes using the in-game engine (which might involve decisions, dialogue options, etc), they're non-interactive. They were once commonplace in RPGs, such as Final Fantasy games from Final Fantasy VII onwards, but due to ever-advancing technology, the difference in visual quality between in-game graphics and pre-rendered cutscenes has been continually diminishing and RPGs have been trending towards fewer and fewer pre-rendered cutscenes. If you're planning to write an RPG script and you want advice about how to write pre-rendered cutscenes, then please pay close attention.

Firstly, in your script, write PRE-RENDERED CUTSCENE at the beginning of the cutscene and END PRE-RENDERED CUTSCENE at the end of the cutscene. You'll need to keep pre-rendered cutscenes *quite* succinct – aim for no longer than 2 and a half minutes per pre-rendered cutscene, and only use such cutscenes for vitally important moments in the story. Focus on plot/action and have minimal use of dialogue in pre-rendered cutscenes. Try to keep the combined length of all pre-rendered cutscenes in the game around 1 hour, 1 and a half hours at most.

- If you're offered an Option Agreement or contract to produce a project, read it thoroughly and don't be afraid to request the document written in layman terms.

- Identify and update obsolete information in your own files - "Reduce, Reuse, Recycle" in loose terms.

I hope these tips help! Best of luck with your writing career!

Polish Plans and Replacement Episodes Plan

Recently, after becoming emboldened (in a positive way) by how well a '6 Week Polish Plan' (polish as in nail polish) turned out for a movie script I'd been stuck on for years (a script containing the Lords of Heaven I mentioned earlier, which I'll call UBA for clarity), I came up with a plan to rework episodes 17-24 of a particular series into one of the movies for that series. I set myself a '3 Week Polish Plan' to tweak the resulting movie script (which I'll call 'PG' for clarity), even printing out the script to go through the dialogue with a fine-tooth comb.

I also brainstormed ideas for 8 'replacement episodes' ('replacement eps' for short) to fill in the gap in the episode count created by the migrated content (by migrating the previous content for episodes 17-24 to a movie, it's separate from the series episode count).

There were three storylines that worked well together, so I kept those in the movie, and removed about 2 episodes worth of some other content which kind of clashed with those storylines and moved it into some of the new episodes where it could be interspersed.

I cut about 5 pages or so of content from PG's script that were only slowing down the pacing, and one idea which was poorly executed was reworked into the storyline of one of the replacement episodes (with much better execution of the idea, of course!). I think about two or three lines of dialogue from the 5 cut pages I liked enough to re-use in one of the replacement episodes, but there wasn't really anything else in those 5 pages worth re-using (I'm usually very conversative when it comes to cutting content from scripts – if it improves pacing or overall quality of the script [particularly with a movie script], I might cut content from a script, but otherwise, I'll rarely cut content).

The replacement episodes were much more efficient use of screen time than the content that was migrated to the movie script, and I was able to explore the different races' religions and mythology further as well as further develop conlangs for some of those races. The replacement episodes were also closer to the series' 'voice' than the content reworked into PG since I was *much* more experienced when I wrote them than I was when I wrote the content in the movie script. I was even able to improve foreshadowing of later episodes – foreshadowing that was not present in even the tweaked version of PG's script!

PG developed a much stronger sense of identity as well as much more of a sense of humour. The movie's pace is a little on the slow side due to originally being written as 8 episodes of a half-hour show and the 5 pages of cut content was originally to pad out screen time in certain episodes.

I ended up printing off PG's script twice – once to make significant tweaks (understandably, the printout got messy with all the corrected dialogue that I wrote in pen), and a second time to make more subtle tweaks (with a much less messy printout). I probably won't require a third printout as there's not much room for dialogue to improve further.

I'm fairly pleased by how my movie and replacement episodes plan turned out – I initially set myself the goal of completing most of the replacement ep scripts in January 2022, but five days of writing were missed due to hot weather (I have a 'hot weather policy' regarding writing – if the temperature on the day is 35 degrees or over, I won't do writing on that day [Australia tends to have very hot summers]), and it took a little longer than expected as I was juggling some other projects (I finished the replacement eps in May 2022, but some proof-reads might be required).

As for the script with the 6 Week Polish Plan, UBA, an audience review for an animated Mortal Kombat movie gave me the 'Eureka!' moment I needed, and I focused on fleshing out the characters' backstories – allowing about 3 pages of flashbacks per character (one character, due to the storyline I chose for that character's flashbacks, ran longer than expected and ended up having something like 5 or 6 pages of flashbacks, though).

I also extensively tweaked the dialogue in that script, and the combination of fleshing out the characters and the tweaked dialogue helped that script to come alive.

I *did* need to tweak and update two episodes of the series set after the 'replacement episodes' in order to include references to those replacement episodes – a narration/prologue where the parts mentioning PG were condensed to 1-2 sentences instead of most of the narration, and I succinctly alluded to the plot each of the replacement episodes in a single sentence, even including a small amount of alliteration; and the other episode condensed the references to PG and included brief mentions of the replacement episodes. This was necessary so that it avoided a situation where the replacement episodes weren't mentioned in any later episodes, which would have made it much more obvious, from the audience's perspective, that the replacement episodes had been added later. PG still has the original prologue/narration for that part of the series and the first of the replacement episodes simply mentions the events of PG has having happened several weeks ago – so the 3 Week Polish Plan and Replacement Episodes Plan is not entirely seamless, but it works.

You might not ever need to come up with a plan as ambitious as my combined 3 Week Polish Plan and Replacement Episodes Plan, but hopefully it gives you an idea of the possibilities for reworking content to improve the quality of a series (note that this applies mostly to a TV series rather than other creative formats).

Have confidence in even your early projects!

Logline And Synopsis

I've read online that when reading queries, screenwriting managers, producers, and the like tend to look for loglines and synopses and if your queries lack either or both, your chances of receiving a response are significantly lower. If you've never even tried to write either loglines or synopses, let alone both, then you might be unknowingly (and unintentionally) sabotaging your attempts to get responses from creative industry gatekeepers.

A logline is 1-2 sentences that sum up the premise of your movie script/TV series, video game, etc. Don't confuse loglines with taglines – taglines are a catchy or memorable phrase that you might see on a poster or flyer for a movie. Keep in mind that the premise is not the full plot, it's more like the *concept* of the plot. It might also help to think of the premise as the dominant plot elements.

A synopsis is a brief summary of plot that covers the major

points (or 'plot beats', if you prefer) of that creative work. Generally, a synopsis will not go into exhaustive detail about *minor* plot points.

I've read online that a synopsis can be anywhere from a few paragraphs to a full page, but avoid writing a synopsis longer than 1 page by any means necessary. If you can comfortably summarise your movie's plot in 2-3 paragraphs, then try to aim for that length with your synopsis.

When writing loglines, do *not* use character's names and instead use adjectives relating to that character, such as their personality, their occupation, gender, nationality, religion, hobbies, etc. Your loglines should not be asking a question, and should give a rough idea what obstacle(s) the protagonist(s) experience.

Practicing writing 'one-liners' (as mentioned earlier) might be good practice for writing loglines. Something you'll definitely want to avoid when writing loglines is 'waffling'. Any unnecessary 'filler' words should be removed from your loglines – any words that aren't revealing extra information don't belong in a logline.

A well-written synopsis should give an overview of the overall plot without getting too caught up in unnecessary details about events of minor importance and there should be *no* lines of dialogue from the script included in the synopsis. It may be difficult to convey humour in a synopsis without referencing dialogue if your movie script, TV series or video game is a comedy. Conveying humour through humourous situations instead of dialogue might be possible in a synopsis if the description of the plot, when read, sounds like a situation that lends itself to comedy.

If your movie script, TV series or video game *is* a comedy, try roleplaying and imagining that you're an agent, screenwriting manager or producer reading a synopsis from an unproduced writer who has sent you a query email 'out of the blue'. Does the plot the synopsis describes *sound* comedic, as opposed to a drama? Would *you* offer to read that writer's comedy script if *you* were the agent, screenwriting manager or producer?

If you tried that roleplaying exercise, and for whatever reason decided that you would *not* be willing to read a comedy script if *you* were a creative industry gatekeeper, then it could be a sign that either or both the logline and synopsis are not accurately conveying that your script is a comedy. Don't worry too much if that's the case, without referencing dialogue, it can be difficult to convey comedy through only a summary of the premise/plot. Remain calm, and revise either or both your logline and/or your synopsis until you have an accurate reflection of the 'gist' of your comedy script.

Of course, if your movie script, TV series or video game is *not* comedic, it may be much easier to create a compelling logline and/or synopsis.

You probably won't need loglines if you're planning to publish novels, especially if your plans for creativity involve *only* novels and no creative work in any other format, but you *may* still need (a) synopsis/synopses when querying a publisher. If you've planned far enough ahead that you have at least a plot outline for your *next* novel, then go ahead and try writing a synopsis for that novel so that you can offer the publisher more than just the novel you've most recently completed.

A well-written logline and/or synopsis *might* improve your success rate with enquiries. Even a poorly written logline and/or synopsis *should* be better than none!

Creativity Prayers

This mini-chapter contains a few creativity prayers devised specifically for inclusion in this book.

The prayer below is a creativity prayer I devised to assist with improving creativity in parts of the world not normally perceived as 'creative' (with the exception of India). I cannot guarantee or promise any specific outcomes from this prayer, and even if any discernible effect materialises, there may be a significant delay between when the prayer was recited and when effects of this prayer begin to manifest. This prayer was not included in my previous book, T*he Prayer Preparer* as I devised it after *The Prayer Preparer* had already been published.

> "Creator, please do absolutely everything within
> your power, within reason, to promote and nurture
> creativity and spiritual creatives in Germany, Spain,
> Italy, Ukraine, Russia, China, South America/
> Brazil (whichever you believe would be more

useful), Africa, The Middle East, South East Asia and India, and those same places in the Etheric as well and especially. Many thanks."

This next prayer is for promoting and nurturing spiritual creatives in countries that are already highly creative:

"Creator, please promote and nurture spiritual creatives in the U.S, Japan, the U.K, Canada, and France."

A prayer for helping writers find inspiration:

"Creator of All That Is (x3), please now bless [name of writer(s)] with abundant divine inspiration and help him/her/them to craft original, inspired and fresh storylines with memorable characters, memorable villains, and intelligent, meaningful and memorable dialogue."

A prayer for helping comedy writers find inspiration:

"Creator of All That Is (x3), please now bless [name of writer(s)] with abundant divine inspiration and help him/her/them to write original, inspired and fresh humour with memorable characters, memorable jokes, and frequent laugh-out-loud moments in his/her/their creative works."

Creativity Prayers

A general prayer for creativity and inspiration:

"Creator of All That Is (x3), please
let the uninspired be inspired and let
the 'creatives' be creative still."

Prayers for finding inspiration/improve projects:

"Creator of All That Is (x3), please let
me receive unending divine inspiration
for my creative writing."

"Creator of All That Is (x3), please let me
receive inspiration for any creative projects
I am experiencing writer's block with."

"Creator of All That Is (x3), please help
me to improve any creative projects
that I feel unsatisfied with."

Miscellaneous creativity prayers:

"Creator of All That Is (x3), from now on, please
let there be fewer new crime shows, murder
mysteries and reality TV shows produced
and let there be more new creative works
based on mythology, especially obscure or
underrepresented mythologies. Many thanks."

"Creator of All That Is (x3), please let
there be more new songs with divinely

inspired lyrics and fewer new songs without divinely inspired lyrics. Many thanks."

"Creator of All That Is (x3), please let the most deserving unproduced writers succeed at getting creative works produced. Many thanks."

"Creator of All That Is (x3), please let there be a much higher number of U.S TV shows that are based on mythology. Many thanks."

"Creator of All That Is (x3), please let there be a higher number of video game franchises based on mythology, especially obscure or underrepresented mythologies."

"Creator of All That Is (x3), please help young writers diversify their creative oeuvre in terms of variety of content and genre."

"Creator of All That Is (x3), please help unproduced writers develop perseverance with their writing."

"Creator of All That Is (x3), please develop a detailed plan for helping unproduced writers succeed."

If you enjoyed and/or benefitted from this book, a review would be greatly appreciated and would help others to benefit from this book. Please consider spending a few moments of your time to write a review to help other aspiring writers know if it is worth purchasing and spending some moments of their time to read. It's my sincere hope and goal with this book to empower as many writers as possible and help them achieve their full creative potential, please help that hope and goal be realised.

www.ingramcontent.com/pod-product-compliance
Lightning Source LLC
Chambersburg PA
CBHW031403040426
42444CB00005B/398